THIS IS YOUR **PASSBOOK**® FOR ...

RECREATION AIDE

NATIONAL LEARNING CORPORATION®
passbooks.com

PASSBOOK® SERIES

THE *PASSBOOK® SERIES* has been created to prepare applicants and candidates for the ultimate academic battlefield – the examination room.

At some time in our lives, each and every one of us may be required to take an examination – for validation, matriculation, admission, qualification, registration, certification, or licensure.

Based on the assumption that every applicant or candidate has met the basic formal educational standards, has taken the required number of courses, and read the necessary texts, the *PASSBOOK® SERIES* furnishes the one special preparation which may assure passing with confidence, instead of failing with insecurity. Examination questions – together with answers – are furnished as the basic vehicle for study so that the mysteries of the examination and its compounding difficulties may be eliminated or diminished by a sure method.

This book is meant to help you pass your examination provided that you qualify and are serious in your objective.

The entire field is reviewed through the huge store of content information which is succinctly presented through a provocative and challenging approach – the question-and-answer method.

A climate of success is established by furnishing the correct answers at the end of each test.

You soon learn to recognize types of questions, forms of questions, and patterns of questioning. You may even begin to anticipate expected outcomes.

You perceive that many questions are repeated or adapted so that you can gain acute insights, which may enable you to score many sure points.

You learn how to confront new questions, or types of questions, and to attack them confidently and work out the correct answers.

You note objectives and emphases, and recognize pitfalls and dangers, so that you may make positive educational adjustments.

Moreover, you are kept fully informed in relation to new concepts, methods, practices, and directions in the field.

You discover that you arre actually taking the examination all the time: you are preparing for the examination by "taking" an examination, not by reading extraneous and/or supererogatory textbooks.

In short, this PASSBOOK®, used directedly, should be an important factor in helping you to pass your test.

RECREATION AIDE

DUTIES
Assists the recreation assistants, workers and supervisors in the planning and execution of various types of recreation programs; performs related duties as required.

SCOPE OF THE EXAMINATION
The written test will cover knowledge, skills and/or abilities in such areas as:

1. Fundamentals of recreation activities;
2. Organizing and conducting recreation activities;
3. Organizing data into tables and records; and
4. Preparation of written material.

HOW TO TAKE A TEST

I. YOU MUST PASS AN EXAMINATION

A. *WHAT EVERY CANDIDATE SHOULD KNOW*

Examination applicants often ask us for help in preparing for the written test. What can I study in advance? What kinds of questions will be asked? How will the test be given? How will the papers be graded?

As an applicant for a civil service examination, you may be wondering about some of these things. Our purpose here is to suggest effective methods of advance study and to describe civil service examinations.

Your chances for success on this examination can be increased if you know how to prepare. Those "pre-examination jitters" can be reduced if you know what to expect. You can even experience an adventure in good citizenship if you know why civil service exams are given.

B. *WHY ARE CIVIL SERVICE EXAMINATIONS GIVEN?*

Civil service examinations are important to you in two ways. As a citizen, you want public jobs filled by employees who know how to do their work. As a job seeker, you want a fair chance to compete for that job on an equal footing with other candidates. The best-known means of accomplishing this two-fold goal is the competitive examination.

Exams are widely publicized throughout the nation. They may be administered for jobs in federal, state, city, municipal, town or village governments or agencies.

Any citizen may apply, with some limitations, such as the age or residence of applicants. Your experience and education may be reviewed to see whether you meet the requirements for the particular examination. When these requirements exist, they are reasonable and applied consistently to all applicants. Thus, a competitive examination may cause you some uneasiness now, but it is your privilege and safeguard.

C. *HOW ARE CIVIL SERVICE EXAMS DEVELOPED?*

Examinations are carefully written by trained technicians who are specialists in the field known as "psychological measurement," in consultation with recognized authorities in the field of work that the test will cover. These experts recommend the subject matter areas or skills to be tested; only those knowledges or skills important to your success on the job are included. The most reliable books and source materials available are used as references. Together, the experts and technicians judge the difficulty level of the questions.

Test technicians know how to phrase questions so that the problem is clearly stated. Their ethics do not permit "trick" or "catch" questions. Questions may have been tried out on sample groups, or subjected to statistical analysis, to determine their usefulness.

Written tests are often used in combination with performance tests, ratings of training and experience, and oral interviews. All of these measures combine to form the best-known means of finding the right person for the right job.

II. HOW TO PASS THE WRITTEN TEST

A. NATURE OF THE EXAMINATION

To prepare intelligently for civil service examinations, you should know how they differ from school examinations you have taken. In school you were assigned certain definite pages to read or subjects to cover. The examination questions were quite detailed and usually emphasized memory. Civil service exams, on the other hand, try to discover your present ability to perform the duties of a position, plus your potentiality to learn these duties. In other words, a civil service exam attempts to predict how successful you will be. Questions cover such a broad area that they cannot be as minute and detailed as school exam questions.

In the public service similar kinds of work, or positions, are grouped together in one "class." This process is known as *position-classification*. All the positions in a class are paid according to the salary range for that class. One class title covers all of these positions, and they are all tested by the same examination.

B. FOUR BASIC STEPS

1) Study the announcement

How, then, can you know what subjects to study? Our best answer is: "Learn as much as possible about the class of positions for which you've applied." The exam will test the knowledge, skills and abilities needed to do the work.

Your most valuable source of information about the position you want is the official exam announcement. This announcement lists the training and experience qualifications. Check these standards and apply only if you come reasonably close to meeting them.

The brief description of the position in the examination announcement offers some clues to the subjects which will be tested. Think about the job itself. Review the duties in your mind. Can you perform them, or are there some in which you are rusty? Fill in the blank spots in your preparation.

Many jurisdictions preview the written test in the exam announcement by including a section called "Knowledge and Abilities Required," "Scope of the Examination," or some similar heading. Here you will find out specifically what fields will be tested.

2) Review your own background

Once you learn in general what the position is all about, and what you need to know to do the work, ask yourself which subjects you already know fairly well and which need improvement. You may wonder whether to concentrate on improving your strong areas or on building some background in your fields of weakness. When the announcement has specified "some knowledge" or "considerable knowledge," or has used adjectives like "beginning principles of..." or "advanced ... methods," you can get a clue as to the number and difficulty of questions to be asked in any given field. More questions, and hence broader coverage, would be included for those subjects which are more important in the work. Now weigh your strengths and weaknesses against the job requirements and prepare accordingly.

3) Determine the level of the position

Another way to tell how intensively you should prepare is to understand the level of the job for which you are applying. Is it the entering level? In other words, is this the position in which beginners in a field of work are hired? Or is it an intermediate or advanced level? Sometimes this is indicated by such words as "Junior" or "Senior" in the class title. Other jurisdictions use Roman numerals to designate the level – Clerk I, Clerk II, for example. The word "Supervisor" sometimes appears in the title. If the level is not indicated by the title, check the description of duties. Will you be working under very close supervision, or will you have responsibility for independent decisions in this work?

4) Choose appropriate study materials

Now that you know the subjects to be examined and the relative amount of each subject to be covered, you can choose suitable study materials. For beginning level jobs, or even advanced ones, if you have a pronounced weakness in some aspect of your training, read a modern, standard textbook in that field. Be sure it is up to date and has general coverage. Such books are normally available at your library, and the librarian will be glad to help you locate one. For entry-level positions, questions of appropriate difficulty are chosen – neither highly advanced questions, nor those too simple. Such questions require careful thought but not advanced training.

If the position for which you are applying is technical or advanced, you will read more advanced, specialized material. If you are already familiar with the basic principles of your field, elementary textbooks would waste your time. Concentrate on advanced textbooks and technical periodicals. Think through the concepts and review difficult problems in your field.

These are all general sources. You can get more ideas on your own initiative, following these leads. For example, training manuals and publications of the government agency which employs workers in your field can be useful, particularly for technical and professional positions. A letter or visit to the government department involved may result in more specific study suggestions, and certainly will provide you with a more definite idea of the exact nature of the position you are seeking.

III. KINDS OF TESTS

Tests are used for purposes other than measuring knowledge and ability to perform specified duties. For some positions, it is equally important to test ability to make adjustments to new situations or to profit from training. In others, basic mental abilities not dependent on information are essential. Questions which test these things may not appear as pertinent to the duties of the position as those which test for knowledge and information. Yet they are often highly important parts of a fair examination. For very general questions, it is almost impossible to help you direct your study efforts. What we can do is to point out some of the more common of these general abilities needed in public service positions and describe some typical questions.

1) General information

Broad, general information has been found useful for predicting job success in some kinds of work. This is tested in a variety of ways, from vocabulary lists to questions about current events. Basic background in some field of work, such as sociology or economics, may be sampled in a group of questions. Often these are principles which have become familiar to most persons through exposure rather than through formal training. It is difficult to advise you how to study for these questions; being alert to the world around you is our best suggestion.

2) Verbal ability

An example of an ability needed in many positions is verbal or language ability. Verbal ability is, in brief, the ability to use and understand words. Vocabulary and grammar tests are typical measures of this ability. Reading comprehension or paragraph interpretation questions are common in many kinds of civil service tests. You are given a paragraph of written material and asked to find its central meaning.

3) Numerical ability

Number skills can be tested by the familiar arithmetic problem, by checking paired lists of numbers to see which are alike and which are different, or by interpreting charts and graphs. In the latter test, a graph may be printed in the test booklet which you are asked to use as the basis for answering questions.

4) Observation

A popular test for law-enforcement positions is the observation test. A picture is shown to you for several minutes, then taken away. Questions about the picture test your ability to observe both details and larger elements.

5) Following directions

In many positions in the public service, the employee must be able to carry out written instructions dependably and accurately. You may be given a chart with several columns, each column listing a variety of information. The questions require you to carry out directions involving the information given in the chart.

6) Skills and aptitudes

Performance tests effectively measure some manual skills and aptitudes. When the skill is one in which you are trained, such as typing or shorthand, you can practice. These tests are often very much like those given in business school or high school courses. For many of the other skills and aptitudes, however, no short-time preparation can be made. Skills and abilities natural to you or that you have developed throughout your lifetime are being tested.

Many of the general questions just described provide all the data needed to answer the questions and ask you to use your reasoning ability to find the answers. Your best preparation for these tests, as well as for tests of facts and ideas, is to be at your physical and mental best. You, no doubt, have your own methods of getting into an exam-taking mood and keeping "in shape." The next section lists some ideas on this subject.

IV. KINDS OF QUESTIONS

Only rarely is the "essay" question, which you answer in narrative form, used in civil service tests. Civil service tests are usually of the short-answer type. Full instructions for answering these questions will be given to you at the examination. But in case this is your first experience with short-answer questions and separate answer sheets, here is what you need to know:

1) Multiple-choice Questions

Most popular of the short-answer questions is the "multiple choice" or "best answer" question. It can be used, for example, to test for factual knowledge, ability to solve problems or judgment in meeting situations found at work.

A multiple-choice question is normally one of three types—

- It can begin with an incomplete statement followed by several possible endings. You are to find the one ending which *best* completes the statement, although some of the others may not be entirely wrong.
- It can also be a complete statement in the form of a question which is answered by choosing one of the statements listed.
- It can be in the form of a problem – again you select the best answer.

Here is an example of a multiple-choice question with a discussion which should give you some clues as to the method for choosing the right answer:

When an employee has a complaint about his assignment, the action which will *best* help him overcome his difficulty is to
A. discuss his difficulty with his coworkers
B. take the problem to the head of the organization
C. take the problem to the person who gave him the assignment
D. say nothing to anyone about his complaint

In answering this question, you should study each of the choices to find which is best. Consider choice "A" – Certainly an employee may discuss his complaint with fellow employees, but no change or improvement can result, and the complaint remains unresolved. Choice "B" is a poor choice since the head of the organization probably does not know what assignment you have been given, and taking your problem to him is known as "going over the head" of the supervisor. The supervisor, or person who made the assignment, is the person who can clarify it or correct any injustice. Choice "C" is, therefore, correct. To say nothing, as in choice "D," is unwise. Supervisors have and interest in knowing the problems employees are facing, and the employee is seeking a solution to his problem.

2) True/False Questions

The "true/false" or "right/wrong" form of question is sometimes used. Here a complete statement is given. Your job is to decide whether the statement is right or wrong.

SAMPLE: A roaming cell-phone call to a nearby city costs less than a non-roaming call to a distant city.

This statement is wrong, or false, since roaming calls are more expensive.
This is not a complete list of all possible question forms, although most of the others are variations of these common types. You will always get complete directions for

answering questions. Be sure you understand *how* to mark your answers – ask questions until you do.

V. RECORDING YOUR ANSWERS

Computer terminals are used more and more today for many different kinds of exams.

For an examination with very few applicants, you may be told to record your answers in the test booklet itself. Separate answer sheets are much more common. If this separate answer sheet is to be scored by machine – and this is often the case – it is highly important that you mark your answers correctly in order to get credit.

An electronic scoring machine is often used in civil service offices because of the speed with which papers can be scored. Machine-scored answer sheets must be marked with a pencil, which will be given to you. This pencil has a high graphite content which responds to the electronic scoring machine. As a matter of fact, stray dots may register as answers, so do not let your pencil rest on the answer sheet while you are pondering the correct answer. Also, if your pencil lead breaks or is otherwise defective, ask for another.

Since the answer sheet will be dropped in a slot in the scoring machine, be careful not to bend the corners or get the paper crumpled.

The answer sheet normally has five vertical columns of numbers, with 30 numbers to a column. These numbers correspond to the question numbers in your test booklet. After each number, going across the page are four or five pairs of dotted lines. These short dotted lines have small letters or numbers above them. The first two pairs may also have a "T" or "F" above the letters. This indicates that the first two pairs only are to be used if the questions are of the true-false type. If the questions are multiple choice, disregard the "T" and "F" and pay attention only to the small letters or numbers.

Answer your questions in the manner of the sample that follows:

32. The largest city in the United States is
    A. Washington, D.C.
    B. New York City
    C. Chicago
    D. Detroit
    E. San Francisco

1) Choose the answer you think is best. (New York City is the largest, so "B" is correct.)
2) Find the row of dotted lines numbered the same as the question you are answering. (Find row number 32)
3) Find the pair of dotted lines corresponding to the answer. (Find the pair of lines under the mark "B.")
4) Make a solid black mark between the dotted lines.

VI. BEFORE THE TEST

Common sense will help you find procedures to follow to get ready for an examination. Too many of us, however, overlook these sensible measures. Indeed, nervousness and fatigue have been found to be the most serious reasons why applicants fail to do their best on civil service tests. Here is a list of reminders:

- Begin your preparation early – Don't wait until the last minute to go scurrying around for books and materials or to find out what the position is all about.
- Prepare continuously – An hour a night for a week is better than an all-night cram session. This has been definitely established. What is more, a night a week for a month will return better dividends than crowding your study into a shorter period of time.
- Locate the place of the exam – You have been sent a notice telling you when and where to report for the examination. If the location is in a different town or otherwise unfamiliar to you, it would be well to inquire the best route and learn something about the building.
- Relax the night before the test – Allow your mind to rest. Do not study at all that night. Plan some mild recreation or diversion; then go to bed early and get a good night's sleep.
- Get up early enough to make a leisurely trip to the place for the test – This way unforeseen events, traffic snarls, unfamiliar buildings, etc. will not upset you.
- Dress comfortably – A written test is not a fashion show. You will be known by number and not by name, so wear something comfortable.
- Leave excess paraphernalia at home – Shopping bags and odd bundles will get in your way. You need bring only the items mentioned in the official notice you received; usually everything you need is provided. Do not bring reference books to the exam. They will only confuse those last minutes and be taken away from you when in the test room.
- Arrive somewhat ahead of time – If because of transportation schedules you must get there very early, bring a newspaper or magazine to take your mind off yourself while waiting.
- Locate the examination room – When you have found the proper room, you will be directed to the seat or part of the room where you will sit. Sometimes you are given a sheet of instructions to read while you are waiting. Do not fill out any forms until you are told to do so; just read them and be prepared.
- Relax and prepare to listen to the instructions
- If you have any physical problem that may keep you from doing your best, be sure to tell the test administrator. If you are sick or in poor health, you really cannot do your best on the exam. You can come back and take the test some other time.

VII. AT THE TEST

The day of the test is here and you have the test booklet in your hand. The temptation to get going is very strong. Caution! There is more to success than knowing the right answers. You must know how to identify your papers and understand variations in the type of short-answer question used in this particular examination. Follow these suggestions for maximum results from your efforts:

1) Cooperate with the monitor

The test administrator has a duty to create a situation in which you can be as much at ease as possible. He will give instructions, tell you when to begin, check to see that you are marking your answer sheet correctly, and so on. He is not there to guard you, although he will see that your competitors do not take unfair advantage. He wants to help you do your best.

2) Listen to all instructions

Don't jump the gun! Wait until you understand all directions. In most civil service tests you get more time than you need to answer the questions. So don't be in a hurry. Read each word of instructions until you clearly understand the meaning. Study the examples, listen to all announcements and follow directions. Ask questions if you do not understand what to do.

3) Identify your papers

Civil service exams are usually identified by number only. You will be assigned a number; you must not put your name on your test papers. Be sure to copy your number correctly. Since more than one exam may be given, copy your exact examination title.

4) Plan your time

Unless you are told that a test is a "speed" or "rate of work" test, speed itself is usually not important. Time enough to answer all the questions will be provided, but this does not mean that you have all day. An overall time limit has been set. Divide the total time (in minutes) by the number of questions to determine the approximate time you have for each question.

5) Do not linger over difficult questions

If you come across a difficult question, mark it with a paper clip (useful to have along) and come back to it when you have been through the booklet. One caution if you do this – be sure to skip a number on your answer sheet as well. Check often to be sure that you have not lost your place and that you are marking in the row numbered the same as the question you are answering.

6) Read the questions

Be sure you know what the question asks! Many capable people are unsuccessful because they failed to *read* the questions correctly.

7) Answer all questions

Unless you have been instructed that a penalty will be deducted for incorrect answers, it is better to guess than to omit a question.

8) Speed tests

It is often better NOT to guess on speed tests. It has been found that on timed tests people are tempted to spend the last few seconds before time is called in marking answers at random – without even reading them – in the hope of picking up a few extra points. To discourage this practice, the instructions may warn you that your score will be "corrected" for guessing. That is, a penalty will be applied. The incorrect answers will be deducted from the correct ones, or some other penalty formula will be used.

9) Review your answers

If you finish before time is called, go back to the questions you guessed or omitted to give them further thought. Review other answers if you have time.

10) Return your test materials

If you are ready to leave before others have finished or time is called, take ALL your materials to the monitor and leave quietly. Never take any test material with you. The monitor can discover whose papers are not complete, and taking a test booklet may be grounds for disqualification.

VIII. EXAMINATION TECHNIQUES

1) Read the general instructions carefully. These are usually printed on the first page of the exam booklet. As a rule, these instructions refer to the timing of the examination; the fact that you should not start work until the signal and must stop work at a signal, etc. If there are any *special* instructions, such as a choice of questions to be answered, make sure that you note this instruction carefully.

2) When you are ready to start work on the examination, that is as soon as the signal has been given, read the instructions to each question booklet, underline any key words or phrases, such as *least*, *best*, *outline*, *describe* and the like. In this way you will tend to answer as requested rather than discover on reviewing your paper that you *listed without describing*, that you selected the *worst* choice rather than the *best* choice, etc.

3) If the examination is of the objective or multiple-choice type – that is, each question will also give a series of possible answers: A, B, C or D, and you are called upon to select the best answer and write the letter next to that answer on your answer paper – it is advisable to start answering each question in turn. There may be anywhere from 50 to 100 such questions in the three or four hours allotted and you can see how much time would be taken if you read through all the questions before beginning to answer any. Furthermore, if you come across a question or group of questions which you know would be difficult to answer, it would undoubtedly affect your handling of all the other questions.

4) If the examination is of the essay type and contains but a few questions, it is a moot point as to whether you should read all the questions before starting to answer any one. Of course, if you are given a choice – say five out of seven and the like – then it is essential to read all the questions so you can eliminate the two that are most difficult. If, however, you are asked to answer all the questions, there may be danger in trying to answer the easiest one first because you may find that you will spend too much time on it. The best technique is to answer the first question, then proceed to the second, etc.

5) Time your answers. Before the exam begins, write down the time it started, then add the time allowed for the examination and write down the time it must be completed, then divide the time available somewhat as follows:

- If 3-1/2 hours are allowed, that would be 210 minutes. If you have 80 objective-type questions, that would be an average of 2-1/2 minutes per question. Allow yourself no more than 2 minutes per question, or a total of 160 minutes, which will permit about 50 minutes to review.
- If for the time allotment of 210 minutes there are 7 essay questions to answer, that would average about 30 minutes a question. Give yourself only 25 minutes per question so that you have about 35 minutes to review.

6) The most important instruction is to *read each question* and make sure you know what is wanted. The second most important instruction is to *time yourself properly* so that you answer every question. The third most important instruction is to *answer every question*. Guess if you have to but include something for each question. Remember that you will receive no credit for a blank and will probably receive some credit if you write something in answer to an essay question. If you guess a letter – say "B" for a multiple-choice question – you may have guessed right. If you leave a blank as an answer to a multiple-choice question, the examiners may respect your feelings but it will not add a point to your score. Some exams may penalize you for wrong answers, so in such cases *only*, you may not want to guess unless you have some basis for your answer.

7) Suggestions
   a. Objective-type questions
      1. Examine the question booklet for proper sequence of pages and questions
      2. Read all instructions carefully
      3. Skip any question which seems too difficult; return to it after all other questions have been answered
      4. Apportion your time properly; do not spend too much time on any single question or group of questions
      5. Note and underline key words – *all, most, fewest, least, best, worst, same, opposite,* etc.
      6. Pay particular attention to negatives
      7. Note unusual option, e.g., unduly long, short, complex, different or similar in content to the body of the question
      8. Observe the use of "hedging" words – *probably, may, most likely,* etc.
      9. Make sure that your answer is put next to the same number as the question
      10. Do not second-guess unless you have good reason to believe the second answer is definitely more correct
      11. Cross out original answer if you decide another answer is more accurate; do not erase until you are ready to hand your paper in
      12. Answer all questions; guess unless instructed otherwise
      13. Leave time for review

   b. Essay questions
      1. Read each question carefully
      2. Determine exactly what is wanted. Underline key words or phrases.
      3. Decide on outline or paragraph answer

4. Include many different points and elements unless asked to develop any one or two points or elements
5. Show impartiality by giving pros and cons unless directed to select one side only
6. Make and write down any assumptions you find necessary to answer the questions
7. Watch your English, grammar, punctuation and choice of words
8. Time your answers; don't crowd material

8) Answering the essay question

Most essay questions can be answered by framing the specific response around several key words or ideas. Here are a few such key words or ideas:

M's: manpower, materials, methods, money, management
P's: purpose, program, policy, plan, procedure, practice, problems, pitfalls, personnel, public relations
    a. Six basic steps in handling problems:
        1. Preliminary plan and background development
        2. Collect information, data and facts
        3. Analyze and interpret information, data and facts
        4. Analyze and develop solutions as well as make recommendations
        5. Prepare report and sell recommendations
        6. Install recommendations and follow up effectiveness

    b. Pitfalls to avoid
        1. *Taking things for granted* – A statement of the situation does not necessarily imply that each of the elements is necessarily true; for example, a complaint may be invalid and biased so that all that can be taken for granted is that a complaint has been registered
        2. *Considering only one side of a situation* – Wherever possible, indicate several alternatives and then point out the reasons you selected the best one
        3. *Failing to indicate follow up* – Whenever your answer indicates action on your part, make certain that you will take proper follow-up action to see how successful your recommendations, procedures or actions turn out to be
        4. *Taking too long in answering any single question* – Remember to time your answers properly

IX. AFTER THE TEST

Scoring procedures differ in detail among civil service jurisdictions although the general principles are the same. Whether the papers are hand-scored or graded by machine we have described, they are nearly always graded by number. That is, the person who marks the paper knows only the number – never the name – of the applicant. Not until all the papers have been graded will they be matched with names. If other tests, such as training and experience or oral interview ratings have been given, scores will be combined. Different parts of the examination usually have different weights. For example, the written test might count 60 percent of the final grade, and a rating of training and experience 40 percent. In many jurisdictions, veterans will have a certain number of points added to their grades.

After the final grade has been determined, the names are placed in grade order and an eligible list is established. There are various methods for resolving ties between those who get the same final grade – probably the most common is to place first the name of the person whose application was received first. Job offers are made from the eligible list in the order the names appear on it. You will be notified of your grade and your rank as soon as all these computations have been made. This will be done as rapidly as possible.

People who are found to meet the requirements in the announcement are called "eligibles." Their names are put on a list of eligible candidates. An eligible's chances of getting a job depend on how high he stands on this list and how fast agencies are filling jobs from the list.

When a job is to be filled from a list of eligibles, the agency asks for the names of people on the list of eligibles for that job. When the civil service commission receives this request, it sends to the agency the names of the three people highest on this list. Or, if the job to be filled has specialized requirements, the office sends the agency the names of the top three persons who meet these requirements from the general list.

The appointing officer makes a choice from among the three people whose names were sent to him. If the selected person accepts the appointment, the names of the others are put back on the list to be considered for future openings.

That is the rule in hiring from all kinds of eligible lists, whether they are for typist, carpenter, chemist, or something else. For every vacancy, the appointing officer has his choice of any one of the top three eligibles on the list. This explains why the person whose name is on top of the list sometimes does not get an appointment when some of the persons lower on the list do. If the appointing officer chooses the second or third eligible, the No. 1 eligible does not get a job at once, but stays on the list until he is appointed or the list is terminated.

X. HOW TO PASS THE INTERVIEW TEST

The examination for which you applied requires an oral interview test. You have already taken the written test and you are now being called for the interview test – the final part of the formal examination.

You may think that it is not possible to prepare for an interview test and that there are no procedures to follow during an interview. Our purpose is to point out some things you can do in advance that will help you and some good rules to follow and pitfalls to avoid while you are being interviewed.

What is an interview supposed to test?

The written examination is designed to test the technical knowledge and competence of the candidate; the oral is designed to evaluate intangible qualities, not readily measured otherwise, and to establish a list showing the relative fitness of each candidate – as measured against his competitors – for the position sought. Scoring is not on the basis of "right" and "wrong," but on a sliding scale of values ranging from "not passable" to "outstanding." As a matter of fact, it is possible to achieve a relatively low score without a single "incorrect" answer because of evident weakness in the qualities being measured.

Occasionally, an examination may consist entirely of an oral test – either an individual or a group oral. In such cases, information is sought concerning the technical knowledges and abilities of the candidate, since there has been no written examination for this purpose. More commonly, however, an oral test is used to supplement a written examination.

Who conducts interviews?

The composition of oral boards varies among different jurisdictions. In nearly all, a representative of the personnel department serves as chairman. One of the members of the board may be a representative of the department in which the candidate would work. In some cases, "outside experts" are used, and, frequently, a businessman or some other representative of the general public is asked to serve. Labor and management or other special groups may be represented. The aim is to secure the services of experts in the appropriate field.

However the board is composed, it is a good idea (and not at all improper or unethical) to ascertain in advance of the interview who the members are and what groups they represent. When you are introduced to them, you will have some idea of their backgrounds and interests, and at least you will not stutter and stammer over their names.

What should be done before the interview?

While knowledge about the board members is useful and takes some of the surprise element out of the interview, there is other preparation which is more substantive. It *is* possible to prepare for an oral interview – in several ways:

1) Keep a copy of your application and review it carefully before the interview

This may be the only document before the oral board, and the starting point of the interview. Know what education and experience you have listed there, and the sequence and dates of all of it. Sometimes the board will ask you to review the highlights of your experience for them; you should not have to hem and haw doing it.

2) Study the class specification and the examination announcement

Usually, the oral board has one or both of these to guide them. The qualities, characteristics or knowledges required by the position sought are stated in these documents. They offer valuable clues as to the nature of the oral interview. For example, if the job involves supervisory responsibilities, the announcement will usually indicate that knowledge of modern supervisory methods and the qualifications of the candidate as a supervisor will be tested. If so, you can expect such questions, frequently in the form of a hypothetical situation which you are expected to solve. NEVER go into an oral without knowledge of the duties and responsibilities of the job you seek.

3) Think through each qualification required

Try to visualize the kind of questions you would ask if you were a board member. How well could you answer them? Try especially to appraise your own knowledge and background in each area, *measured against the job sought*, and identify any areas in which you are weak. Be critical and realistic – do not flatter yourself.

4) Do some general reading in areas in which you feel you may be weak

For example, if the job involves supervision and your past experience has NOT, some general reading in supervisory methods and practices, particularly in the field of human relations, might be useful. Do NOT study agency procedures or detailed manuals. The oral board will be testing your understanding and capacity, not your memory.

5) Get a good night's sleep and watch your general health and mental attitude

You will want a clear head at the interview. Take care of a cold or any other minor ailment, and of course, no hangovers.

What should be done on the day of the interview?

Now comes the day of the interview itself. Give yourself plenty of time to get there. Plan to arrive somewhat ahead of the scheduled time, particularly if your appointment is in the fore part of the day. If a previous candidate fails to appear, the board might be ready for you a bit early. By early afternoon an oral board is almost invariably behind schedule if there are many candidates, and you may have to wait. Take along a book or magazine to read, or your application to review, but leave any extraneous material in the waiting room when you go in for your interview. In any event, relax and compose yourself.

The matter of dress is important. The board is forming impressions about you – from your experience, your manners, your attitude, and your appearance. Give your personal appearance careful attention. Dress your best, but not your flashiest. Choose conservative, appropriate clothing, and be sure it is immaculate. This is a business interview, and your appearance should indicate that you regard it as such. Besides, being well groomed and properly dressed will help boost your confidence.

Sooner or later, someone will call your name and escort you into the interview room. *This is it.* From here on you are on your own. It is too late for any more preparation. But remember, you asked for this opportunity to prove your fitness, and you are here because your request was granted.

What happens when you go in?

The usual sequence of events will be as follows: The clerk (who is often the board stenographer) will introduce you to the chairman of the oral board, who will introduce you to the other members of the board. Acknowledge the introductions before you sit down. Do not be surprised if you find a microphone facing you or a stenotypist sitting by. Oral interviews are usually recorded in the event of an appeal or other review.

Usually the chairman of the board will open the interview by reviewing the highlights of your education and work experience from your application – primarily for the benefit of the other members of the board, as well as to get the material into the record. Do not interrupt or comment unless there is an error or significant misinterpretation; if that is the case, do not hesitate. But do not quibble about insignificant matters. Also, he will usually ask you some question about your education, experience or your present job – partly to get you to start talking and to establish the interviewing "rapport." He may start the actual questioning, or turn it over to one of the other members. Frequently, each member undertakes the questioning on a particular area, one in which he is perhaps most competent, so you can expect each member to participate in the examination. Because time is limited, you may also expect some rather abrupt switches in the direction the questioning takes, so do not be upset by it. Normally, a board member will not pursue a single line of questioning unless he discovers a particular strength or weakness.

After each member has participated, the chairman will usually ask whether any member has any further questions, then will ask you if you have anything you wish to add. Unless you are expecting this question, it may floor you. Worse, it may start you off on an extended, extemporaneous speech. The board is not usually seeking more information. The question is principally to offer you a last opportunity to present further qualifications or to indicate that you have nothing to add. So, if you feel that a significant qualification or characteristic has been overlooked, it is proper to point it out in a sentence or so. Do not compliment the board on the thoroughness of their examination – they have been sketchy, and you know it. If you wish, merely say, "No thank you, I have nothing further to add." This is a point where you can "talk yourself out" of a good impression or fail to present an important bit of information. Remember, *you close the interview yourself.*

The chairman will then say, "That is all, Mr. _____, thank you." Do not be startled; the interview is over, and quicker than you think. Thank him, gather your belongings and take your leave. Save your sigh of relief for the other side of the door.

How to put your best foot forward

Throughout this entire process, you may feel that the board individually and collectively is trying to pierce your defenses, seek out your hidden weaknesses and embarrass and confuse you. Actually, this is not true. They are obliged to make an appraisal of your qualifications for the job you are seeking, and they want to see you in your best light. Remember, they must interview all candidates and a non-cooperative candidate may become a failure in spite of their best efforts to bring out his qualifications. Here are 15 suggestions that will help you:

1) Be natural – Keep your attitude confident, not cocky

If you are not confident that you can do the job, do not expect the board to be. Do not apologize for your weaknesses, try to bring out your strong points. The board is interested in a positive, not negative, presentation. Cockiness will antagonize any board member and make him wonder if you are covering up a weakness by a false show of strength.

2) Get comfortable, but don't lounge or sprawl

Sit erectly but not stiffly. A careless posture may lead the board to conclude that you are careless in other things, or at least that you are not impressed by the importance of the occasion. Either conclusion is natural, even if incorrect. Do not fuss with your clothing, a pencil or an ashtray. Your hands may occasionally be useful to emphasize a point; do not let them become a point of distraction.

3) Do not wisecrack or make small talk

This is a serious situation, and your attitude should show that you consider it as such. Further, the time of the board is limited – they do not want to waste it, and neither should you.

4) Do not exaggerate your experience or abilities

In the first place, from information in the application or other interviews and sources, the board may know more about you than you think. Secondly, you probably will not get away with it. An experienced board is rather adept at spotting such a situation, so do not take the chance.

5) If you know a board member, do not make a point of it, yet do not hide it

Certainly you are not fooling him, and probably not the other members of the board. Do not try to take advantage of your acquaintanceship – it will probably do you little good.

6) Do not dominate the interview

Let the board do that. They will give you the clues – do not assume that you have to do all the talking. Realize that the board has a number of questions to ask you, and do not try to take up all the interview time by showing off your extensive knowledge of the answer to the first one.

7) Be attentive

You only have 20 minutes or so, and you should keep your attention at its sharpest throughout. When a member is addressing a problem or question to you, give him your undivided attention. Address your reply principally to him, but do not exclude the other board members.

8) Do not interrupt

A board member may be stating a problem for you to analyze. He will ask you a question when the time comes. Let him state the problem, and wait for the question.

9) Make sure you understand the question

Do not try to answer until you are sure what the question is. If it is not clear, restate it in your own words or ask the board member to clarify it for you. However, do not haggle about minor elements.

10) Reply promptly but not hastily

A common entry on oral board rating sheets is "candidate responded readily," or "candidate hesitated in replies." Respond as promptly and quickly as you can, but do not jump to a hasty, ill-considered answer.

11) Do not be peremptory in your answers

A brief answer is proper – but do not fire your answer back. That is a losing game from your point of view. The board member can probably ask questions much faster than you can answer them.

12) Do not try to create the answer you think the board member wants

He is interested in what kind of mind you have and how it works – not in playing games. Furthermore, he can usually spot this practice and will actually grade you down on it.

13) Do not switch sides in your reply merely to agree with a board member

Frequently, a member will take a contrary position merely to draw you out and to see if you are willing and able to defend your point of view. Do not start a debate, yet do not surrender a good position. If a position is worth taking, it is worth defending.

14) Do not be afraid to admit an error in judgment if you are shown to be wrong

The board knows that you are forced to reply without any opportunity for careful consideration. Your answer may be demonstrably wrong. If so, admit it and get on with the interview.

15) Do not dwell at length on your present job

The opening question may relate to your present assignment. Answer the question but do not go into an extended discussion. You are being examined for a *new* job, not your present one. As a matter of fact, try to phrase ALL your answers in terms of the job for which you are being examined.

Basis of Rating

Probably you will forget most of these "do's" and "don'ts" when you walk into the oral interview room. Even remembering them all will not ensure you a passing grade. Perhaps you did not have the qualifications in the first place. But remembering them will help you to put your best foot forward, without treading on the toes of the board members.

Rumor and popular opinion to the contrary notwithstanding, an oral board wants you to make the best appearance possible. They know you are under pressure – but they also want to see how you respond to it as a guide to what your reaction would be under the pressures of the job you seek. They will be influenced by the degree of poise you display, the personal traits you show and the manner in which you respond.

ABOUT THIS BOOK

This book contains tests divided into Examination Sections. Go through each test, answering every question in the margin. At the end of each test look at the answer key and check your answers. On the ones you got wrong, look at the right answer choice and learn. Do not fill in the answers first. Do not memorize the questions and answers, but understand the answer and principles involved. On your test, the questions will likely be different from the samples. Questions are changed and new ones added. If you understand these past questions you should have success with any changes that arise. Tests may consist of several types of questions. We have additional books on each subject should more study be advisable or necessary for you. Finally, the more you study, the better prepared you will be. This book is intended to be the last thing you study before you walk into the examination room. Prior study of relevant texts is also recommended. NLC publishes some of these in our Fundamental Series. Knowledge and good sense are important factors in passing your exam. Good luck also helps. So now study this Passbook, absorb the material contained within and take that knowledge into the examination. Then do your best to pass that exam.

———

EXAMINATION SECTION

EXAMINATION SECTION
TEST 1

DIRECTIONS: Each question or incomplete statement is followed by several suggested answers or completions. Select the one that BEST answers the question or completes the statement. *PRINT THE LETTER OF THE CORRECT ANSWER IN THE SPACE AT THE RIGHT.*

1. Of the following, the MOST desirable help that can be rendered by volunteer assistants in the playground program is in

    A.   preparing materials
    B.   making individual corrections
    C.   teaching game skills
    D.   inspecting for safety hazards

1.____

2. Of the following, the procedure which is MOST essential in maintaining good discipline in the playgrounds is to

    A.   establish a definite set of rules
    B.   provide interesting games and activities for all groups
    C.   punish offenders promptly
    D.   establish peer leadership

2.____

3. Of the following, the LEAST important factor to be considered in program planning is

    A.   available facilities
    B.   total program objectives
    C.   skill of participants
    D.   availability of volunteer leadership

3.____

4. Of the following, the one that is indispensable for the enjoyment of MOST forms of recreation is

    A.   expert performance
    B.   seriousness of purpose
    C.   a reasonable degree of proficiency
    D.   considerable effort

4.____

5. Of the following, the MOST important factor in ensuring safety on trips taken by playground groups is

    A.   selecting the safest means of transportation
    B.   establishing rules of conduct with the participants before the trip is started
    C.   checking on the attendance of the participants frequently during the trip
    D.   making sure that the trip is concluded on time

5.____

6. Of the following, a common social characteristic of children in the twelve-to-fourteen-year-old group is that they

    A.   often feel misunderstood
    B.   accept adult leadership easily
    C.   are rarely interested in other people's ideas
    D.   seek independence from the peer group

6.____

7. Of the following statements, the one which represents the MOST acceptable statement concerning the relationship of active to passive activities in the playground program is: 7.____

    A. Interest and age groupings should determine the stress that should be given to either active or passive activities
    B. Active and passive activities should each be accorded the same amount of time
    C. Passive activities should be used as a means of providing an interesting rest period
    D. Passive activities should be given emphasis during inclement weather

8. Of the following, the one which represents the BEST statement of policy concerning the inclusion of volleyball in the program of the playground is: 8.____

    A. Volleyball should be a constant activity since every child may participate success-fully
    B. After a period of orientation and motivation, volleyball should be included only if students show an enthusiasm for it
    C. Early exposure, followed by interesting competition, should make volleyball inter-esting to all
    D. The nature of the game is such as to indicate that only the girls are likely to be interested in volleyball over a period of time

9. One group game generates an exceptionally interesting participation on the part of both boys and girls. 9.____
Of the following recommendations to the teacher, which is preferred?

    A. Continue playing the game as long as children are interested.
    B. Rearrange the planned schedule so as to devote unlimited additional time to it.
    C. Continue playing until a majority wants another activity.
    D. Resume the activity after discontinuing it before interest lags.

10. Of the following, a PRIMARY reason for holding a softball tournament among teams of students who attend the playground is that 10.____

    A. competition becomes more meaningful and interesting
    B. tournaments are attractive to spectators
    C. an overall winner can be identified
    D. it keeps many children from getting into trouble

11. Of the following, the MOST significant reason for including tennis instruction in the play-ground program is that it 11.____

    A. provides an excellent all-around exercise
    B. has continuing lifetime value for many individuals
    C. provides many students with a meaningful challenge
    D. is a genteel sport and tends to raise the cultural sights of students

12. Of the following, the MOST effective procedure in bringing children of varying social background into effective social interaction is 12.____

    A. arranging periodic discussions with harmonious interaction as the objective
    B. arranging for the parents of the different groups to meet together
    C. convincing the leadership of these groups that cooperative activity is desirable
    D. arranging for adults to talk to these children

13. Of the following, the MOST important factor in ensuring the success of a tournament   13.____
conducted in the playground is

    A.   equalizing the potential of teams through a careful selection of team personnel
    B.   providing only the most competent officials
    C.   involving students intimately in publicity for the tournament
    D.   giving teams attractive names

14. Of the following, the LEAST important consideration in organizing groups of children for   14.____
various physical activities is

    A.   age   B.   athletic ability
    C.   individual interest   D.   size

15. Of the following, the procedure which is MOST likely to ensure the success of a rainy-   15.____
day program in the playground is

    A.   planning schedules for such a day before the season starts
    B.   arranging for moving pictures to consume the time during the rainy period
    C.   planning for such a day with a group of children representative of the entire group
    D.   consulting with the teacher in charge in ascertaining the nature of programs that
         have been successful

16. Of the following, the factor which is likely to contribute MOST to making a special events   16.____
program in the playground a success is to

    A.   provide the teacher in charge of the activity with sufficient time to plan
    B.   organize an adequate number of student committees and groups to deal with all
         aspects of the plan
    C.   send written invitations to parents to visit
    D.   offer a prize to the student who has contributed most

17. Of the following, the LEAST important factor in the effective selection of physical activi-   17.____
ties for the playground program is the

    A.   interests of the majority
    B.   seasonal factor in various sports
    C.   abilities of the group
    D.   availability of supplies and facilities

18. Of the following, the LEAST important factor in setting up equipment in a game room is   18.____
to

    A.   provide for grouping according to the interests of various age levels
    B.   consider the safety hazards inherent in the arrangement
    C.   facilitate teacher supervision
    D.   divide activities according to different interests of boys and girls

19. Of the following, the one which is likely to be MOST successful in assisting children   19.____
attending the program to grow socially is

    A.   periodic suggestions and admonitions concerning the rights of others
    B.   group discussions about the rights of minorities
    C.   a program of activities that involves social interplay
    D.   a summary at the end of each day stressing the help given one another

20. Of the following, the procedure which is likely to be LEAST important in improving student attendance in the playground is

    20.____

    A. keeping a roll book and checking attendance morning and afternoon
    B. conferring individually with children who tend to be absent
    C. providing activities based on their appeal to student interests
    D. being pleasant to children at all times

21. The assistance of adult volunteers in the vacation playground program may be used profitably in all of the following capacities EXCEPT

    21.____

    A. publicizing center activities
    B. assisting with registration procedures
    C. supervising children on a trip
    D. taking full charge of the physical activities program

22. Of the following, the BEST procedure for the teacher concerned with developing a meaningful outdoor program of physical activities is to

    22.____

    A. concentrate on one activity at a time, e.g., the playing of softball
    B. provide a variety of activities in keeping with the limitations of space and facilities
    C. insist that each student participate in each activity on a rotational basis to ensure broad experience
    D. establish definitive plans at the beginning of the season and adhere to them

23. Of the following, the PRIME purpose of a novelty game is to

    23.____

    A. afford a sense of success to the non-athletic pupil
    B. appeal to competitive instincts of children
    C. require little space or equipment
    D. provide an easily conducted activity where discipline problems rarely develop

24. Of the following, the LEAST important purpose of a bulletin board newspaper in the playground is to

    24.____

    A. make available some of the values of a small group experience
    B. provide recognition and success for some
    C. increase the interest in playground events
    D. develop insight into news reporting as a possible vocation

25. Of the following, the statement which BEST explains the attitude of thirteen year olds toward coeducational activities is:

    25.____

    A. Coeducational activities of a social nature appeal but many are shy about participating in them
    B. Girls enjoy such activities, but boys generally do not
    C. Coeducational activities appeal to boys and girls at this age principally in a party atmosphere
    D. Boys and girls are not interested in the same activities at this age

26. The problem of identifying student leaders for the playground program involves the question of the chronological age group likely to produce effective leaders.
Of the following, which is the statement MOST likely to apply concerning leadership?

    26.____

A. Leadership potentials have little relationship to chronological age.
B. The twelve-to-fourteen year old group is ready for opportunities of leadership
C. Leaders should be chosen from among the oldest students in the group
D. Every child has leadership potential

27. In addition to teaching children how to play games provided for the game room area, it is essential that the teacher   27.____

    A. instruct in the proper use of equipment
    B. provide copies of essential rules of the game
    C. organize student leaders to conduct games
    D. suggest how to choose opposing players

28. Of the following, the recommended procedure to follow when playground equipment has been broken is to   28.____

    A. report it at once to the custodian
    B. organize student committees to repair it
    C. remove the equipment
    D. advise students not to use it

29. Of the following, the PRIMARY objective of the playground teacher in introducing a new group game should be to   29.____

    A. develop initially a thorough understanding of the rules so as to minimize conflict
    B. start the group promptly after an understanding of the objectives and the basic rules of the game
    C. develop and practice skills to be used in the game
    D. determine those who are interested so that the others may be given some other activity

30. Of the following, the BEST way to obtain *good discipline* in playground activities as contrasted with *order* is by   30.____

    A. meeting each infraction with prompt and precise action
    B. establishing an understanding of the rationale for regulations
    C. appealing to students through their parents or others
    D. rewarding good conduct in a tangible way

31. Of the following, the BEST way to help a child who displays an undesirable emotional reaction to losing a game is by   31.____

    A. reprimanding him
    B. showing him his error after he has *cooled off*
    C. barring him temporarily from competition
    D. ignoring him completely

32. Of the following, the procedure which is of PRIMARY importance in the conduct of a game room is to   32.____

    A. make sure that no equipment is lost
    B. provide for a system of rotation so that all can participate
    C. avoid the use of too many activities so that supervision is difficult
    D. arrange for boys and girls to participate together

33. Of the following, the BEST technique in maintaining attendance in the game room at a high level is to   33.____

    A. announce the schedule well in advance
    B. make the room attractive
    C. organize tournaments in various activities
    D. provide ample bulletin board space

34. Of the following, the BEST procedure to follow in organizing and planning a game room program is to   34.____

    A. consult the teacher-in-charge to determine those activities which have previously proven to be of interest
    B. consider the suggestions made by authorities concerning activities that have been successful
    C. visit other playgrounds to determine the elements of the program that have been successful
    D. involve students in the planning of the program

35. Of the following, the factor which is considered to be the LEAST important in the conduct of a successful game room program is   35.____

    A. a spirit of friendliness
    B. respect for others
    C. an opportunity for self-expression
    D. a spirit of competition

36. Of the following, the MAJOR reason for using pupils in leadership roles in the playground program is to   36.____

    A. assist the teacher in the organization and administration of a broad program
    B. give expression to the leadership potential of students
    C. keep students satisfied with the way matters are handled
    D. keep some students from becoming problems

37. Of the following, the procedure which is of GREATEST importance to the game room teacher planning a series of lessons in table tennis is   37.____

    A. deciding the age level of the children to be included
    B. ascertaining the names of children who are interested
    C. planning the progression of skills to be taught
    D. determining when to start the actual participation of students

38. It is recommended that the game room in a playground be organized so as to   38.____

    A. separate boys and girls
    B. divide students according to the interests of various age levels
    C. allow the teacher to bring groups together readily
    D. provide for easy transfer from one activity to another

39. Of the following, the MOST difficult problem in program planning for the playground is   39.____

    A. providing for small groups within the total program
    B. separating boys' and girls' activities

C. making full use of special facilities
D. encouraging skillful participants to undertake leadership roles

40. Of the following, the MOST serious hazard in a game room area is likely to be   40.____

    A. running   B. insufficient ventilation
    C. overcrowding   D. age differences

41. Of the following, the LEAST significant value of the games offered in the game room is in   41.____

    A. learning to take turns
    B. accepting the decision of others
    C. widening the circle of friends
    D. learning to compete with more able opponents

42. In bowling, the MAXIMUM individual score that it is possible to achieve in one game is   42.____

    A. 150   B. 200   C. 250   D. 300

43. All of the following apply to the playing of circle stride ball EXCEPT: 43.____

    A. Players stand with feet astride, touching neighbors' feet
    B. One player stands in the center of a circle
    C. A player may move his feet to block a ball
    D. Sometimes the ball is thrown into the circle from outside it

44. All of the following skills are useful in playing the game *Endball* EXCEPT   44.____

    A. throwing   B. catching
    C. dribbling   D. pivoting

45. In badminton, the server serves   45.____

    A. until hand is out
    B. until a point is scored
    C. until the winning point is scored
    D. five times in succession

46. Badminton and tennis are LEAST alike in the   46.____

    A. shape of the playing surface
    B. use of nets
    C. use of rackets
    D. method of scoring

47. In regulation play, a match in badminton consists of winning _____ out of _____   47.____
    games.

    A. two; three   B. three; four
    C. three; five   D. four; six

48. A *bird* in badminton falling on a boundary line is considered   48.____

    A. *In* court
    B. *Out* of court
    C. *In* or *Out* dependent on whether the play is a service or volley
    D. as requiring a replay if a service

49. Of the following games, the one which requires the LEAST athletic skill is   49._____

    A. volleyball   B. dodgeball
    C. shuffleboard   D. captain ball

50. Of the following scores in tennis, the one which does NOT indicate the completion of a   50._____
set is

    A. 9-8   B. 6-4   C. 13-11   D. 7-5

51. The type of tournament that provides for competition through challenge is the   51._____

    A. round robin   B. consolation
    C. ladder   D. elimination

52. In order to complete a round robin type tournament with eight teams, the number of   52._____
games to be played is

    A. 16   B. 24   C. 28   D. 32

53. In volleyball, the manner of rotation of players in position for service is   53._____

    A. front and back   B. counterclockwise
    C. clockwise   D. laterally

54. Safety hazards are implicit in all forms of athletic activities.   54._____
Of the following, the LEAST important consideration in minimizing these hazards is

    A. a daily inspection of facilities and equipment
    B. the arrangement of activities in the playground
    C. the establishment of regulations concerning costume
    D. a mimeographed list of hazards distributed to participants

55. In volleyball, the *underarm* serve is preferred because it   55._____

    A. is easier to learn
    B. offers a maximum of control
    C. offers as much speed as other serves
    D. is harder to return

56. A player serving in volleyball must comply with all of the following rules EXCEPT: 56._____

    A. Both feet must be behind the back line
    B. The ball must be hit with an open hand
    C. The ball must go clearly over the net
    D. Each member of the team serves in turn

57. In organizing teams for a volleyball tournament in the playground, it is advisable to   57._____
arrange for a number of players and a few substitutes for each team.
The basic number, exclusive of substitutes, should be

    A. 6   B. 8   C. 10   D. 12

58. Of the following, the factor which is likely to be MOST productive in making volleyball an   58._____
interesting and continuing activity among children is

    A. teacher participation
    B. adequate initial motivation

    C.   individual and group success in playing the game
    D.   frequent opportunities to play the game

59.   In table tennis, when the score is 20-20, a player   59._____

    A.   must score two successive points to win
    B.   must score the 21st point to win
    C.   can score the winning point only while serving
    D.   must score 5 additional points to win

60.   Of the following, the essential difference between singles and doubles play in table ten-   60._____
      nis is

    A.   number of points served consecutively by any one player
    B.   area to which the serve must be hit
    C.   number of points constituting a game
    D.   rules governing a *let*

61.   In paddle tennis, when both players have won two points, the score is   61._____

    A.   three all   B.   advantage in or out
    C.   thirty all   D.   deuce

62.   In table tennis, a player loses a point in all of the following situations EXCEPT when he   62._____

    A.   fails to make a good service
    B.   permits anything on his person to touch the supports for the net while playing the
        ball
    C.   permits his free hand to touch the playing surface while playing the ball
    D.   moves from behind the table in returning a ball

63.   In a tie game at *20-all* in table tennis, the serve   63._____

    A.   continues to be alternated at every five additional points
    B.   is alternated on every subsequent point
    C.   is alternated after every two additional points
    D.   is made by the loser of each subsequent point

64.   Of the following, the MOST common error in table tennis is   64._____

    A.   failing to be properly poised for the stroke before contact with the ball
    B.   standing too close to the table
    C.   hitting the ball too softly
    D.   confusing the backhand and forehand shots

65.   In treating a victim of nosebleed, of the following, the LEAST effective procedure is to   65._____

    A.   have the victim lie down immediately
    B.   press the nostrils firmly together
    C.   apply a large, cold, wet cloth to the nose
    D.   pack the nose gently with gauze

66.   Sharp cuts that tend to bleed freely are called   66._____

    A.   lacerated wounds   B.   abrasions
    C.   puncture wounds   D.   incised wounds

67. The group of symptoms which BEST describes a case of shock is:　　　　67.＿＿＿

    A. Headache, face flushed, pupils of eyes pinpointed
    B. Pupils of eyes dilated, face cold and moist, pulse weak
    C. Extreme thirst, chills, breathing deep and slow
    D. Reactions irrational, skin dry and warm, pulse slow

68. The score 15-13 could indicate the final score of a completed game in any of the follow-　68.＿＿＿
    ing activities EXCEPT

    A. baseball　　　　　　　　　　　B. football
    C. table tennis　　　　　　　　　　D. badminton

69. In performing the back pressure-arm lift method of artificial respiration, the operator　　69.＿＿＿
    should _____ of the victim.

    A. kneel at the head　　　　　　　B. straddle both thighs
    C. kneel at either side　　　　　　D. straddle one thigh

70. The overall purpose of the application of heat to a victim in shock is to　　　　70.＿＿＿

    A. cause sweating
    B. prevent a large loss of body heat
    C. increase the body's temperature
    D. increase the blood circulation

71. A condition which may result from a deficiency of vitamin C is known as　　　71.＿＿＿

    A. beri-beri　　　B. rickets　　　C. scurvy　　　D. impetigo

72. The game in which the winner is determined by the LOWEST score is　　　72.＿＿＿

    A. bowling　　　B. tennis　　　C. golf　　　D. badminton

73. In shuffleboard, the discs are shot from the　　　　73.＿＿＿

    A. base line　　　　　　　　　　B. end line
    C. 10 off are　　　　　　　　　　D. base of the triangle

74. In shuffleboard, all of the following apply EXCEPT　　　74.＿＿＿

    A. point values go from seven to ten
    B. discs coming to rest between the starting line and the farthest dead line are
       removed before play is continued
    C. if a singles game ends in a tie, each player then plays two discs from one end
    D. a disc which has come to rest in a scoring area may be driven off

75. In shuffleboard, all of the following apply EXCEPT　　　75.＿＿＿

    A. in both singles and doubles, sides alternate in shoving discs
    B. in doubles, partners play at opposite ends of the court
    C. the number of discs used by each side is four in singles and six in doubles
    D. a game consists of fifty points

KEY (CORRECT ANSWERS)

1.	A	16.	B	31.	B	46.	D	61.	C
2.	B	17.	B	32.	B	47.	A	62.	D
3.	D	18.	D	33.	C	48.	A	63.	B
4.	C	19.	C	34.	D	49.	C	64.	A
5.	B	20.	A	35.	D	50.	A	65.	A
6.	A	21.	D	36.	B	51.	C	66.	D
7.	B	22.	B	37.	C	52.	C	67.	B
8.	B	23.	A	38.	B	53.	C	68.	C
9.	D	24.	D	39.	A	54.	D	69.	A
10.	A	25.	A	40.	A	55.	B	70.	B
11.	B	26.	B	41.	D	56.	B	71.	C
12.	C	27.	A	42.	D	57.	A	72.	C
13.	A	28.	C	43.	C	58.	C	73.	C
14.	D	29.	B	44.	C	59.	A	74.	C
15.	C	30.	B	45.	A	60.	B	75.	C

TEST 2

DIRECTIONS: Each question or incomplete statement is followed by several suggested answers or completions. Select the one that BEST answers the question or completes the statement. *PRINT THE LETTER OF THE CORRECT ANSWER IN THE SPACE AT THE RIGHT.*

1. Of the following, the BEST statement of principle concerned with the conduct of the physical activities period in the playground is that   1.____

   A. emphasis should be given to team activities
   B. only intramural as opposed to inter playground competition should be encouraged
   C. each period of physical activities should provide a balance between instructional time and *big muscle activity* time
   D. boys should be given more *big muscle* activities than girls

2. Of the following, the MOST important function of the teacher in the playgrounds is   2.____

   A. officiating at various athletic contests
   B. insuring equality of opportunities of participation
   C. interesting students in a variety of activities
   D. gaining the cooperation of parents

3. Of the following, the LEAST important guiding principle in insuring the success of an athletic competition is to   3.____

   A. equalize as far as possible the athletic potential of each team in the make up of its participants
   B. provide as many opportunities for inter-team competition as possible
   C. provide adequate officiating by having the teacher officiate
   D. provide for effective leadership for each team

4. Of the following, the MOST important factor in insuring safe participation in the activities of the playground is   4.____

   A. a preliminary inspection of the facilities by the teacher each day before the program begins
   B. posting rules and regulations concerned with safety
   C. properly warning students about safety hazards before activities begin
   D. exercising continuing supervision of activities

5. Of the following, the one which is considered to be the MOST important responsibility of the playground teacher is   5.____

   A. planning and conducting activities so as to satisfy the play interests of the majority of children
   B. suggesting new and different activities
   C. insuring the physical growth and development of each child
   D. checking to insure adequate attendance

6. Of the following, the factor MOST apt to result in good discipline in the playground is   6.____

   A. peer leadership
   B. positive teacher direction

C. excellent administrative procedure
D. an interesting program of activities

7. Of the following, the LEAST important reason for including a physical activity program in the playgrounds is that it

    7.____

    A. helps develop body organs
    B. builds muscle tone
    C. establishes desirable social attitudes
    D. provides satisfaction in *winning*

8. Of the following, the MOST effective way to improve the attendance in the playground *game room* is by

    8.____

    A. making it a place for reading and browsing
    B. allowing only *quiet* games to be played there
    C. providing a variety of activities, some quiet and others of a semi-active nature
    D. closing down the *active* areas of the playground periodically

9. Of the following, the LEAST important reason for a summer playground program is to

    9.____

    A. keep children off the streets
    B. promote objectives associated with racial integration
    C. broaden the cultural experiences of children
    D. provide meaningful recreational experiences

10. Of the following, the PRIMARY value of motion pictures concerned with sports such as baseball, volleyball, and swimming is to

    10.____

    A. entertain pupils
    B. develop an interest in the activity
    C. show students that results are easy to achieve
    D. assist the teacher to obtain better application

11. The initial attendance in the vacation playground program is raost satisfactory during the first week, but subsequently falls off alarmingly.
The following, the MOST logical explanation is that the

    11.____

    A. teachers have been sympathetic to the problems of the individual
    B. program does not meet the interests of the participants
    C. staff has failed to establish enough competitive activities
    D. participants have found the program too taxing

12. Of the following considerations, the one which is LEAST important in the selection of activities is

    12.____

    A. alternating active and quiet activities
    B. placing emphasis on seasonal considerations
    C. consideration of the mores of the neighborhood served
    D. preventing any one activity from becoming dominant or too absorbing of interest

13. Of the following, the procedure which is MOST likely to be successful in getting the shy child to participate in activities with others is   13.____

    A.   a direct confrontation by the teacher in which the advisability of participating is pointed out
    B.   a patient but persistent encouragement by the teacher
    C.   a conference with the parent held with a view to gaining the parent's assistance
    D.   having older boys or girls talk to the child

14. Student leaders in the playground may be used for all of the following tasks EXCEPT   14.____

    A.   refereeing games
    B.   distributing materials
    C.   acting as assistants in improving skills performed by other students
    D.   opening and closing windows

15. Of the following, the one which is LEAST likely to cause an individual student to become a disciplinary problem in the playground is   15.____

    A.   lack of success in participation
    B.   a sense of insecurity
    C.   a poor relationship at home carried over to the playground
    D.   a dislike of the activities of interest to other children of the same age

16. When the playground teacher finds that a different child hesitates to compete with others in group games, of the following, the BEST procedure to follow is to   16.____

    A.   send for a parent to discuss the matter
    B.   urge the child to be a good sport and participate
    C.   observe the child with a view to determining the cause
    D.   report the matter to the teacher-in-charge

17. Of the following, the method considered to be LEAST effective in the teaching of motor skills is   17.____

    A.   analysis on the part of the teacher
    B.   demonstration by a participant
    C.   imitation
    D.   a verbal description of the skill

18. Of the following, the MAJOR advantage in the use of games of low organization is that   18.____

    A.   relatively unskilled players may gain satisfaction in competing
    B.   the teacher may supervise these more efficiently than other activities
    C.   safety hazards are reduced
    D.   large playground areas may be used more efficiently

19. Of the following elements of successful play experience, the one which is the SLOWEST to develop among young children is   19.____

    A.   interest in participation
    B.   a spirit of competition
    C.   a sense of cooperative enterprise
    D.   absence of undue concern about physical well-being

20. Rainy day programs in the playground should

    A. be limited to quiet games
    B. make effective use of indoor space for both active and quiet games
    C. be such as to limit attendance
    D. consist of assembly programs and the use of motion pictures

20.____

21. Of the following, concerning spectator participation in the activities of the playground, the one which represents the MOST acceptable position is that spectators should be

    A. discouraged
    B. urged to become participants
    C. unnoticed
    D. invited to view special competitions

21.____

22. Of the following, the manner in which parental assistance can be MOST effectively utilized is by

    A. officiating at activities of various kinds
    B. accompanying a group to a museum
    C. preparing a playground newspaper
    D. coaching a dramatics performance

22.____

23. Of the following statements concerning athletic activities to be included in the program of the playground, the one which is the LEAST valid is:

    A. Activities should have *carry-over* values
    B. Only those activities that are devoid of all safety hazards should be included
    C. Activities included can be identified with the interests of chronological age groups
    D. Activities should be related to differing interests based on sex

23.____

24. Of the following, concerning the use of the teacher's whistle, the one which represents the BEST advice is that

    A. the whistle should be used infrequently. When used, it should be blown with incisiveness
    B. a whistle can be used effectively to stop activities and simultaneously to provide *directions*
    C. a whistle should never be blown harshly
    D. the tone and incisiveness of whistle blowing should be varied

24.____

25. Of the following, the factor that is MOST apt to reflect the degree of interest shown by a group of children in a particular game is the

    A. motivation supplied by the teachers
    B. degree of success achieved
    C. length of time of participation
    D. degree of activity provided

25.____

26. Of the following, the PRIMARY value of a well-organized program in the playgrounds is that

    A. disciplinary problems are minimized
    B. it helps to insure a maximum of values for the participants

26.____

C. the time of the participants is fully taken up
D. good attendance is insured

27. A participant under your jurisdiction in the playground abuses equipment several times.   27.____
A typical example of this is *kicking a basketball.*
Of the following, the BEST way to handle the situation after his failure to heed your initial warning is to

A. send for his parents
B. bar him from further participation
C. question him privately in an effort to get him to understand that his actions are wrong
D. report him to the teacher in charge for disciplinary action

28. A teacher assigned to cooperate with you in developing and supervising your program   28.____
frequently *disappears* and fails to accept his responsibilities.
Of the following, the BEST way to handle the situation is to

A. warn him at the earliest opportunity to make certain that this behavior ceases
B. report him to your *immediate superior* with the request that he *speak* to your colleague
C. point out the difficulties that his absence creates for you and your students
D. do the best you can without him and wait for your superior to note his failure to carry out his duties

29. *Assemblies* in the playground schedule of activities are MOST important in that they   29.____

A. provide periods of *quiet* activity
B. develop a community spirit
C. give children important information
D. promote individual interests

30. Of the following, the MOST important result of a well-planned vital program in the play-   30.____
ground is that it

A. contributes to the cultural education of the participants
B. promotes good attendance
C. continues the work of the regular school
D. provides a safe place for children to spend the day

31. Of the following procedures, the one which is considered LEAST valuable in the conduct   31.____
of the daily playground program is

A. calling children together to present and share their experiences of the day
B. holding *assemblies* to present dramatic programs
C. keeping an accurate attendance record for each individual child
D. conducting a preliminary *safety check*

32. Of the following, the LEAST important reason for grouping children on a chronological   32.____
basis is that

A. interests vary
B. safe participation can be promoted

    C. teaching techniques vary with age levels
    D. the teachers' organizational problems are made easier

33. Of the following, the LEAST important principle in conducting a program of movies for   33._____
    showing in the playground program is that

    A. movies should be scheduled for a regular time each week
    B. the movies selected should be entertaining as well as educational
    C. movies should be previewed by the teacher
    D. some of the pictures selected for viewing should be related to the other activities of
        the playground

34. Of the following, the LEAST important consideration in planning the athletic program of   34._____
    the playground is

    A. the facilities that are available
    B. the age groups of the participants
    C. seasonal interests
    D. the skill and ability of the teacher in the activities selected

35. Of the following responsibilities of the playground teacher, the one which is FIRST in   35._____
    importance is to

    A. provide activities for the participation of the maximum number
    B. emphasize big muscle activity
    C. give individual instruction
    D. introduce new activities

36. The playground teacher who is about to introduce a new game will generally find that the   36._____
    BEST way to arouse interest is to

    A. explain the history of the game
    B. outline the object of the game
    C. tell why he enjoyed the game
    D. tell the children that it is a game they will enjoy

37. Of the following, the factor which should exert the LEAST influence on the length of the   37._____
    play period in the playground is

    A. the age of the participants
    B. the degree of interest demonstrated
    C. the number of children and the facilities available
    D. whether it is conducted during the morning or afternoon sessions

38. Of the following, a PRIME objective of the teacher in the vacation playground should be   38._____
    to

    A. develop sound social attributes
    B. teach the rules of group games
    C. entertain children
    D. prevent discord

39. Of the following, the MOST important objective of a trip to a fair by a group of children   39._____
    under your supervision is the

    A. broadening of educational and cultural backgrounds
    B. relieving of the monotony of a daily playground schedule
    C. rewarding of good behavior
    D. learning of how to behave as a member of a group

40. Your playground serves children from two segregated areas. You find that the children   40._____
    tend to remain segregated in the playground.
    Of the following, the BEST way to meet this issue is to

    A. point out to them the importance of effective integration
    B. provide assembly programs with integration as the theme
    C. consult with the parents of the respective groups
    D. provide activities that develop a common sphere of interest

41. Of the following, the MOST effective way to develop good sportsmanship in the play-   41._____
    ground is by

    A. praising evidences of good sportsmanship as these develop
    B. outlining to a group the qualities to be encouraged
    C. showing how good sportsmanship is always rewarded
    D. emphasizing the relative importance of winning as compared to sportsmanship

42. Of the following principles concerning the conduct of the playground program, the one   42._____
    which is of PRIMARY importance is that the

    A. teacher should pre-plan activities
    B. individual participant should be afforded an opportunity to choose activities
    C. activities chosen should be seasonal in nature
    D. outdoor facilities should be used in good weather

43. Of the following, the generally accepted reason for insisting that children be properly   43._____
    instructed in their initial experiences in such activities as golf and tennis is to

    A. prevent them from establishing incorrect habits
    B. provide participation on a safe basis
    C. provide for gradual development in the execution of the skills involved
    D. promote effective interests in the activity

44. The round robin tournament should be used instead of the elimination tournament   44._____

    A. when time is not a factor and the number of teams is small
    B. to provide opportunities for better sportsmanlike participation
    C. when younger participants are involved
    D. when participants want to develop greater skill

45. Of the following, the PRIME importance of tournament programs in team activities is that   45._____
    they

    A. provide a schedule for improving skills of individual participants
    B. develop social skills

    C.   stimulate interest in active participation
    D.   determine a winner

46.   The *ladder* type of tournament is especially useful in conducting competition in   46.____

    A.   table tennis   B.   softball
    C.   basketball   D.   football

47.   Of the following games, the one which requires equipment other than a ball is   47.____

    A.   dodge ball   B.   overhead relay
    C.   call ball   D.   bombardment

48.   All of the following are associated with playing the game of CIRCLE STRIDE BALL   48.____
    EXCEPT

    A.   having adjacent players touch feet
    B.   keeping the hands on the knees during part of the play
    C.   having someone who is *It*
    D.   keeping the body in a semi-crouched position

49.   UNDER-LEGS RELAY, OVERHEAD RELAY, and ZIG-ZAG RELAY are activities of low   49.____
    organization that emphasize particularly skill in

    A.   throwing   B.   passing
    C.   dribbling   D.   shooting

50.   The game AROUND THE WORLD is MOST closely associated with   50.____

    A.   HARE AND HOUNDS   B.   FARMER IN THE DELL
    C.   basketball   D.   SPUD

51.   Of the following team or group activities, the one of GREATEST competitive interest for   51.____
    ten-year-old boys is

    A.   volleyball   B.   table tennis
    C.   softball   D.   snatch the club

52.   In the game of dodgeball, of the following, the factor of LEAST importance in insuring   52.____
    safe participation is the

    A.   size of the circle
    B.   number of participants
    C.   degree of inflation of the ball used
    D.   speed of the participants

53.   Of the following, the activity which provides a child with the BEST opportunity to practice   53.____
    skills in which he has not reached a degree of proficiency is

    A.   the *free enterprise* period
    B.   the playing of a game
    C.   a squad activities period
    D.   an activity in which the individual is assigned leadership roles

54. Which of the following statements is true about the group game known as THREE DEEP?
It is a game

    A. played in a circle formation
    B. that uses *spare* players
    C. employing a *hide and seek* technique
    D. in which the third player throws a ball

54._____

55. Of the following games, the one which employs the LARGEST ball is

    A. volleyball
    C. basketball
    B. pushball
    D. dodgeball

55._____

56. The game END BALL requires

    A. guards and basemen
    B. several basketballs
    C. a large basketball court
    D. at least two referees

56._____

57. Of the following, the MOST important reason for introducing *lead-up* games is that they

    A. engage larger numbers
    B. provide greater satisfaction
    C. tend to sustain greater interest
    D. provide practice in essential skills

57._____

58. Of the following games, the one which employs the FEWEST and SIMPLEST rules is

    A. End Ball
    C. Spud
    B. handball
    D. volleyball

58._____

59. The term *lob* is used in all of the following sports EXCEPT

    A. handball
    C. badminton
    B. tennis
    D. volleyball

59._____

60. A game in which competitors are required to keep *feet touching those of adjacent play-ers* is

    A. Circle Stride Ball
    C. Newcomb
    B. dodgeball
    D. Spud

60._____

61. KEEP-AWAY is a group game that provides practice in

    A. passing a ball
    C. striking a target
    B. tagging opponents
    D. kicking a ball

61._____

62. SPUD is a game that includes all of the following EXCEPT

    A. the numbering of players
    C. running
    B. throwing a ball
    D. selecting partners

62._____

20

63. Of the following relay races, the type which requires a tandem arrangement of competitors is   63._____

    A. Wheelbarrow   B. All Up Relay
    C. Circle Relay   D. Pass Ball Relay

64. In badminton, points are scored   64._____

    A. by either the serving or receiving side
    B. only by the serving side
    C. not until two serves have been made
    D. in a fashion similar to table tennis

65. All of the following are true in the playing of newcomb EXCEPT: 65._____

    A. Teams of 8 to 14 players may be used to advantage
    B. A rope may be used instead of a net
    C. The ball may be relayed between players on the same side
    D. The ball may not touch the net or rope

66. Of the following, the LEAST important reason for including paddle tennis in a playground program is that   66._____

    A. it requires relatively little space
    B. the equipment used is inexpensive and durable
    C. it provides a good background experience for lawn tennis
    D. it is a vigorous activity

67. In badminton, all of the following apply EXCEPT: 67._____

    A. The server may stand outside of his court
    B. The serve must be made with an underhand stroke
    C. If the server makes a fault, he is out
    D. A game may consist of fifteen or twenty-one points

68. In volleyball, a serve is good if it   68._____

    A. is hit by any part of the hand or fist from behind the end line over the net and into the opponent's court
    B. touches the net after being hit by an open hand
    C. is hit by one or both hands over the net and into the opponent's court
    D. is hit over the net from any one of the six player's position, using an open hand

69. All of the following statements are true of the serve in badminton EXCEPT: 69._____

    A. Either an underhand or an overhead swing of the racket is permitted
    B. The server continues to serve until he makes a fault or his opponent scores an *ace*
    C. A successful serve must fall between a *short* and a *long* service line
    D. A shuttle may not be hit twice in succession by the server

70. Of the following, which pair of games is MOST similar in method of play?   70._____

    A. Deck tennis - Newcomb   B. Basketball - soccer
    C. Volleyball - tennis   D. Paddle tennis - handball

71. The American Red Cross recommends that an abrasion be treated by   71.____

    A. applying iodine
    B. covering the wound with gauze
    C. washing the wound with soap and water
    D. applying mercurochrome

72. Of the following, the contagious disease of the skin that the playground teacher should   72.____
recognize in order to protect others is

    A. conjunctivitis
    B. lordosis
    C. Osgood Schlatter's disease
    D. impetigo

73. Of the following, the symptom of heatstroke MOST frequently noted is   73.____

    A. an absence of perspiration
    B. mental confusion
    C. headache
    D. dilated pupils

74. A puncture wound is considered serious from the point of view that   74.____

    A. bleeding may be hard to stop
    B. injury to tissue may be extensive
    C. infection is likely to result
    D. multiple injury may result

75. The method of resuscitation MOST generally accepted today is the _____ method.   75.____

    A. back pressure-arm lift   B. mouth to mouth
    C. Silvester   D. Schaefer

————————

KEY (CORRECT ANSWERS)

1. C	16. C	31. C	46. A	61. A
2. C	17. D	32. D	47. D	62. D
3. C	18. A	33. A	48. D	63. A
4. D	19. C	34. D	49. C	64. B
5. A	20. B	35. A	50. C	65. C
6. D	21. D	36. B	51. C	66. C
7. D	22. B	37. D	52. D	67. A
8. C	23. B	38. A	53. A	68. A
9. A	24. A	39. A	54. A	69. A
10. B	25. B	40. D	55. B	70. A
11. B	26. B	41. A	56. A	71. C
12. D	27. C	42. B	57. D	72. D
13. B	28. C	43. A	58. C	73. A
14. D	29. B	44. A	59. D	74. C
15. D	30. B	45. C	60. A	75. B

———

EXAMINATION SECTION
TEST 1

DIRECTIONS: Each question or incomplete statement is followed by several suggested answers or completions. Select the one that BEST answers the question or completes the statement. *PRINT THE LETTER OF THE CORRECT ANSWER IN THE SPACE AT THE RIGHT.*

1. Of the following, the primary reason for organizing a community council in a center is that it

    1.____

    A. can reflect the interests of members of the community
    B. offers an excellent vehicle for publicity
    C. can coordinate the work of the recreation center
    D. helps staff members to avoid making errors

2. Of the following, the LEAST important factor in insuring the success of a specific element of a recreation center program is

    2.____

    A. the specific evening of the week on which the activity is offered
    B. the degree to which the membership is involved in planning
    C. the preparatory experiences offered
    D. getting the custodian's approval

3. Of the following, the BEST procedure to follow to discourage smoking in lavatories in the centers is to

    3.____

    A. post *no smoking* signs
    B. impose sanctions on offenders
    C. discuss reports on the ill effects of smoking
    D. seek the aid of the custodian

4. As the recreation leader assigned to a large gymnasium, you find that a conflict in time schedule exists between activities planned for the gymnasium and those scheduled for the pool.
   Of the following, the BEST initial step in attempting to resolve this is to

    4.____

    A. refer the matter to a committee of participants
    B. confer with the instructor in charge of the pool
    C. inform the director or recreation supervisor
    D. close the gymnasium during the period in question

5. Of the following, the BEST initial step to take in dealing with pornographic writing on lavatory walls in the center is to

    5.____

    A. make mention of the undesirability of this in the center news release
    B. call the group together for a discussion of the inadvisability of this type of conduct
    C. remove the writing as quickly as possible
    D. try to identify the culprit through the handwriting

6. The instructor assigned to the supervision of the club program should be primarily con-   6.____
   cerned with the

   A. instruction in parliamentary procedure
   B. effective location of clubs in specific rooms
   C. identification of leaders in specific club activities
   D. supervision of attendance

7. Of the following statements, the one which expresses the MOST acceptable viewpoint   7.____
   concerning social dancing in the recreation center is:

   A. Special dances should be held bi-weekly
   B. Dances should not be attempted in difficult areas of the city
   C. An effective program makes provision for teaching social dancing to adolescents
   D. Dances should always be held on Friday evenings

8. Of the following, the one that BEST describes the results of studies of street gangs is that   8.____

   A. the leaders are likely to be psychiatrically disturbed
   B. members join reluctantly and primarily to attain peer approval
   C. the majority of the membership is likely to be interested in social reform
   D. economic deprivation is primarily responsible for their existence

9. Members of the recreation center who habitually linger in the dressing rooms after clos-   9.____
   ing time should

   A. have their membership cancelled after the third offense
   B. be reminded constantly of the need for haste in dressing
   C. be dismissed from the activity areas correspondingly early each evening
   D. be excluded from the center for several evenings

10. Of the following, the CHIEF reason why recreation activities have been more widely par-   10.____
    ticipated in by adults in the last several decades is because of

    A. an increased awareness of their health value
    B. a decreasing length of the work day and an increase in time for leisure
    C. effective publicity campaigns
    D. a greater interest in competition

11. In social dancing, a currently popular dance usually written in 2/8 time is the   11.____

    A. rhumba   B. mambo   C. tango   D. samba

12. In performing the figure, *swing partners,* the _____ step is used.   12.____

    A. buzz   B. chasse   C. galop   D. balance

13. An adolescent should be excluded from the recreation center when he   13.____

    A. disrupts a game
    B. causes a breakdown of the program
    C. damages a piano
    D. is insolent to an instructor

14. At the start of a basketball game, the captain of one of the teams reports to the instructor   14.____
    that a nail is sticking out of the floor under one of the baskets. The instructor gets a ham-
    mer from the custodian and hammers the nail in to remove the hazard.
    In the future, the instructor should

    A. always have a hammer available
    B. have the team captains inspect the court carefully before the beginning of each
       game
    C. be more vigilant in his opening inspection
    D. ask the custodian to check the condition of the floor each day

15. In shuffleboard, match play should be on the basis of _____ games.   15.____

    A. best two out of three   B. best three out of five
    C. winning three straight   D. best four out of seven

16. Of the following, the BEST method of avoiding arguments about rules during basketball   16.____
    games in an intra-center basketball league is to

    A. provide each team with a copy of the current rule book
    B. employ paid referees
    C. make provision for pre-season demonstration clinics
    D. arrange the schedule so that a recreation leader can referee the games

17. When the basketball dribble was first evolved, its primary function was to   17.____

    A. enable a cornered player to get away from his opponent
    B. advance the ball to a scoring position
    C. help set up a play
    D. penetrate a zone defense

18. A mistake commonly made by an inexperienced basketball player in catching a pass is   18.____
    that

    A. he catches the ball and gets set for his next move all in one motion
    B. he starts his next move prior to receiving the ball
    C. he keeps his eye on the ball after it leaves the passer's hands
    D. his hands close about the ball at the moment of contact

19. The MOST difficult basketball pass for an inexperienced player to complete properly is   19.____
    the _____ pass.

    A. bounce   B. underhand
    C. lead   D. long overhand

20. When asked by a center team to referee an inter-center basketball game in a crowded   20.____
    gymnasium, you should refuse primarily because

    A. you may be accused of favoring the home team
    B. if you referee you cannot supervise the activity
    C. by refereeing you deprive an inexperienced referee of the practice in a game situa-
       tion
    D. the recreation center division must supply referees

27

21. Of the following statements regarding the use of a whistle in the gymnasium, the one considered to be MOST appropriate is: 21.____

    A. The whistle may be used as a signal to change activities
    B. The blowing of the whistle should be limited to situations in which attention is desired
    C. A *long* whistle is generally more effective than a *short* whistle
    D. Whistles of different pitch should signify different things

22. Of the following, the BEST approach to a youngster who stands around the gymnasium instead of participating in the activities is to   22.____

    A. impress upon him how much he is missing
    B. try to persuade him to join his friends
    C. invite him to try different activities
    D. inform him that he is not using his time profitably

23. Of the following, the one procedure which potentially is likely to create the MOST serious problem for the activity aide assigned alone to the gymnasium is   23.____

    A. allowing troublemakers to use the facilities
    B. leaving the gymnasium to answer the telephone
    C. making individual members responsible for checking equipment
    D. allowing individuals to participate for too long a period of time

24. Of the following, the factor which is considered LEAST important in contributing to the success of intracenter athletic contests is   24.____

    A. the seasonal nature of activities
    B. effective officiating
    C. the balance of skill as represented in the various teams
    D. a reasonable number of spectators

25. Of the following, the activity in which the services of volunteer leaders can BEST be utilized is in   25.____

    A. shuffleboard and similar games
    B. practice on the running track
    C. volleyball
    D. heavy apparatus activities

KEY (CORRECT ANSWERS)

1.	A	11.	D
2.	D	12.	A
3.	B	13.	B
4.	B	14.	C
5.	C	15.	A
6.	C	16.	C
7.	C	17.	B
8.	B	18.	B
9.	C	19.	D
10.	B	20.	B

21.	B
22.	C
23.	B
24.	D
25.	D

——————

TEST 2

DIRECTIONS: Each question or incomplete statement is followed by several suggested answers or completions. Select the one that BEST answers the question or completes the statement. *PRINT THE LETTER OF THE CORRECT ANSWER IN THE SPACE AT THE RIGHT.*

1. Of the following, the MOST desirable help that can be rendered by volunteer assistants in the recreation center is in

    A. making individual corrections
    B. preparing materials
    C. teaching game skills
    D. inspecting for safety hazards

1.____

2. A condition in which recreation facilities are inadequate is viewed as serious in that adolescents tend to

    A. substitute undesirable activities
    B. become less healthy physically
    C. be inactive
    D. ignore social contacts

2.____

3. Of the following, the BEST rule concerning coeducational activities in the recreation centers is that they should be

    A. limited to the pre-adolescent
    B. limited to club activities and social programs
    C. discussed and planned by boys and girls in consultation with an activity aide sponsor
    D. limited by the director

3.____

4. Of the following, which is the BEST statement concerning the factor of safety in the operation of a recreation center?

    A. Only non-contact sports should be included in the program to insure safety.
    B. When activities are properly conducted, all safety hazards can be avoided.
    C. The placement of activities helps to insure safety.
    D. Posting regulations is the best means to insure safe participation.

4.____

5. The posting of regulations concerning the use of gymnasium equipment is likely to be MOST effective if the

    A. reasons for regulations are discussed in advance of posting
    B. charts are made by participants
    C. printing is artistically attractive
    D. list of regulations covers all contingencies

5.____

6. In golf, the term *bogey* means

    A. par for a hole
    B. one stroke over par for a hole
    C. one stroke under par for two successive holes
    D. two strokes under par for a hole

6.____

7. With regard to golf, it is INCORRECT to state that   7.____

    A. a shot hit with a number 2 iron has a long, low trajectory
    B. the putter may be used only on the green
    C. a wedge is usually used for approach shots
    D. the player of average ability hits his longest shots with the woods

8. In an official badminton game, the option of setting the game rests with the   8.____

    A. home team
    B. team first reaching the tied score
    C. visiting team
    D. team that tied the score

9. In serving the shuttle in badminton, the shuttle is held   9.____

    A. in the manner most suitable to the server
    B. by the tips of the feathers, with the bottom of the shuttle pointing downward
    C. at the bottom of the shuttle, with the feathers toward the net
    D. with the index finger and the thumb, with the feathers pointed downward

10. Of the following strokes in badminton, the one that is NOT dependent upon the flexibility   10.____
of the wrist for proper execution is the _____ stroke.

    A. forehand   B. lift   C. overhead   D. backhand

11. In badminton, the height of the top of the net at the center should be   11.____

    A. 5'3"   B. 5'1"   C. 5'   D. 5'6"

12. In badminton, the server serves   12.____

    A. five times in succession
    B. until a point is scored
    C. until winning points are scored
    D. until hand is out

13. In badminton, as a rule, the MOST important point-winning stroke is the   13.____

    A. service
    B. high, overhead smash downwards
    C. drop shot
    D. clearing shot

14. A winning score in points common to the men's and women's doubles game of badmin-   14.____
ton is

    A. 15   B. 11   C. 18   D. 25

15. Of the following, the oldest game in which a ball is hit across a net is   15.____

    A. table tennis   B. court tennis
    C. badminton   D. paddle tennis

16. Of the following, the LEAST important reason for encouraging basketball teams in the recreation center to acquire appropriate uniforms is to

    A. promote spirited participation
    B. develop team loyalties
    C. present an appearance that impresses visitors
    D. provide identification

16.____

17. Of the following considerations, the one basic to the success of a recreation program is

    A. extensive facilities
    B. an interesting schedule of activities
    C. excellent teaching skill
    D. coeducational activities.

17.____

18. Of the following, the MOST important consideration in planning an athletic program is the

    A. degree to which a specific activity can be enjoyed subsequently
    B. judgment of the instructor as to the value of a specific activity
    C. degree to which individual skills are developed
    D. elimination of all safety hazards

18.____

19. In deciding whether to include volleyball in a recreation center program, the instructor should be guided primarily by the

    A. time that he has available to teach specific skills
    B. degree to which safe participation can be insured
    C. numbers of potential participants
    D. degree to which the game is likely to appeal to potential participants

19.____

20. Mats used in the gymnasium during the evening session should be

    A. left on the floor in convenient locations for use in the day sessions
    B. piled in a corner of the gymnasium
    C. hung on mat hooks, if available
    D. placed on top of apparatus to facilitate subsequent use

20.____

21. Of the following, the main reason for insisting that rubber-soled shoes and an appropriate costume be used by members of the recreation center when using the facilities of the gymnasium is to

    A. maintain a clean floor and to protect street clothing
    B. provide an attractive atmosphere of participation
    C. insure safe participation
    D. identify team members

21.____

22. In a recreation center in which participation in physical activities is sparse and indifferent, the trouble is likely to be found in the

    A. nature of the activities offered
    B. personality of the instructor
    C. failure to publicize the activities
    D. failure to alternate the activities

22.____

23. Coeducational participation should be encouraged in all of the following activities EXCEPT 23.____

    A. swimming   B. badminton
    C. basketball   D. heavy apparatus

24. Of the following, the BEST method for dealing with individual disciplinary problems in the recreation centers is to 24.____

    A. ban the culprits
    B. provide interesting new activities
    C. analyze the causal factors
    D. establish an effective recreation council

25. Clubs meeting as part of the recreation center program should be 25.____

    A. organized by recreation leaders on the basis of previous successes
    B. developed when a sufficient number of members demonstrate interest
    C. diversified to insure all of the objectives of a recreation center program
    D. related to participation in physical activities

KEY (CORRECT ANSWERS)

1.	B		11.	C
2.	A		12.	D
3.	C		13.	A
4.	C		14.	A
5.	A		15.	B
6.	C		16.	C
7.	C		17.	B
8.	B		18.	A
9.	B		19.	D
10.	D		20.	C

21. C
22. A
23. C
24. C
25. B

TEST 3

DIRECTIONS: Each question or incomplete statement is followed by several suggested answers or completions. Select the one that BEST answers the question or completes the statement. *PRINT THE LETTER OF THE CORRECT ANSWER IN THE SPACE AT THE RIGHT.*

1. In a situation in which racial tensions are existent, the recreation center can BEST resolve the inherent difficulties by   1.____

    A. providing activities of common interest
    B. producing a publication in which the problem is discussed
    C. contacting religious leaders
    D. holding social dances

2. Of the following, the MOST practical type of tournament to use in the event of a very large number of entries is the _____ tournament.   2.____

    A. round robin   B. single elimination
    C. ladder   D. pyramid

3. In single-wall handball, if your opponent is playing in close to the wall, the BEST strategy to attempt is a   3.____

    A. kill shot
    B. pass shot down the lanes
    C. crotch ball
    D. high shot that will land near the short line

4. In the event that handball partners (doubles match) change sides during a rally, it is BEST to   4.____

    A. caution one's partner not to repeat this
    B. switch back immediately
    C. keep the newly assumed positions until the game ends
    D. keep the newly assumed positions until the rally ends

5. The number of players on a regulation softball team is   5.____

    A. nine   B. ten   C. eleven   D. twelve

6. In softball, with a runner on first base, if the first baseman catches a grounder and touches first base before the batter does, the runner going to second   6.____

    A. is out if the shortstop catches the first baseman's throw and tags second base
    B. is not allowed to return to first base if he can
    C. must be tagged to be put out
    D. is not permitted to run to third if the first baseman's throw to the shortstop is wild

7. INTRODUCTION TO COMMUNITY RECREATION, a reference book in the recreation field, was prepared for the National Recreation Association by   7.____

    A. George D. Butler   B. Jay B. Nash
    C. Joseph Lee   D. George Hjelte

8. ENCYCLOPEDIA OF SPORTS was written by   8.____

   A. Nat Fleischer   B. Frank G. Menke
   C. Jimmy Powers   D. Grantland Rice

9. The INCORRECT matching of author with title is: 9.____

   A. J.H. Bancroft - GAMES
   B. Mason and Mitchel - BICYCLING AS A HOBBY
   C. S.C. Staley - GAMES, CONTESTS, AND RELAYS
   D. E. Bowers - PARTIES, PLANS, AND PROGRAMS

10. In tennis, the final score for a set is   10.____

   A. 7-5   B. 5-3   C. 8-7   D. 3-2

11. When teaching the serve in tennis, it is POOR coaching technique to emphasize the   11.____

   A. grip   B. stance   C. swing   D. pivot

12. Proper care of a tennis racket does NOT include   12.____

   A. keeping the racket in a waterproof case at all times when not in use
   B. putting a strong press on the racket immediately after use
   C. storing the racket in a dry warm place
   D. applying a thin transparent shellac over the strings to prolong life

13. Of the following, which is TRUE of volleyball?   13.____

   A. Players rotate positions.
   B. Each side serves for five consecutive points always.
   C. The ball is dead when it strikes a player.
   D. A served ball striking the top of the net, then crossing it, is in play.

14. Twenty-one points usually constitute a winning score in all of the following games   14.____
    EXCEPT

   A. handball   B. badminton
   C. volleyball   D. table tennis

15. Of the following, the MOST common error made by beginners in attempting to perform   15.____
    the *backward roll* is an inability to

   A. use the knees effectively
   B. complete the roll
   C. arch the back
   D. coordinate the head and shoulders

16. If ten teams are entered in an elimination tournament, the determination of a winner will   16.____
    require playing _____ games.

   A. seven   B. eight   C. nine   D. ten

17. To acquire skill in specific stunts, all of the following concerning practice are recommended EXCEPT:

    A. Practice should be direct rather than incidental
    B. Long practice periods are more conducive to results than short practice periods
    C. Frequent repetitions are necessary to maintain accuracy that has been gained
    D. Practice that is a result of felt need is more effective than that which is imposed

17._____

18. The *push* pass in basketball is usually made with

    A. legs astride
    B. a step in the direction of the pass
    C. hands held low
    D. knees straight rather than bent

18._____

19. In volleyball, it is illegal for a back position player to

    A. touch a ball hit by another back court teammate
    B. hit the ball with one hand
    C. spike a ball
    D. step into a front court position

19._____

20. The term *setup* in volleyball refers to a(n)

    A. opponent you wish to take advantage of
    B. play in which a back court player passes to front court
    C. play in which a player passes to the attacker
    D. predesigned play

20._____

21. In volleyball, rotation of positions take place

    A. when a team is preparing to start serving
    B. when a team is preparing to receive service
    C. after 3 points have been scored by either team
    D. after 5 minutes of playing time have elapsed

21._____

22. In volleyball, when a served ball strikes an object suspended from the ceiling within the field, the CORRECT ruling is

    A. the ball may be served again
    B. a point is credited to the receiving team
    C. it should be played by the receiving team
    D. the serving team loses the serve

22._____

23. The method of scoring in volleyball is similar to scoring in

    A. handball   B. basketball
    C. table tennis   D. tennis

23._____

24. Of the following terms, the one which applies to volleyball is

    A. fault   B. spike   C. forehand   D. reverse

24._____

25. With regard to respiration, it is CORRECT to state that   25._____

    A. in forced expiration, all of the air in the chest can be expelled
    B. the presence of carbon dioxide in the blood causes the brain area that controls breathing to act
    C. contraction of the muscles of the chest causes expiration
    D. every time one swallows, the windpipe is covered by the uvula

---

KEY (CORRECT ANSWERS)

1.	A		11.	D
2.	B		12.	C
3.	B		13.	A
4.	D		14.	C
5.	A		15.	B
6.	C		16.	C
7.	A		17.	B
8.	B		18.	B
9.	B		19.	C
10.	A		20.	C

21.	B
22.	A
23.	A
24.	B
25.	B

TEST 4

DIRECTIONS: Each question or incomplete statement is followed by several suggested answers or completions. Select the one that BEST answers the question or completes the statement. *PRINT THE LETTER OF THE CORRECT ANSWER IN THE SPACE AT THE RIGHT.*

1. With regard to strains, all of the following are correct EXCEPT

    A. application of heat relieves the pain
    B. rubbing downward on the injured part aids the return flow of blood in the veins
    C. gentle massage helps loosen up the muscles
    D. rest is necessary

    1.____

2. Of the following, the one which is NOT a symptom of shock is

    A. cool, clammy skin   B. weak pulse
    C. flushed face   D. feeling of weakness

    2.____

3. It is INCORRECT to state that the procedure of exercise that causes fatigue is

    A. sarcolactic acid   B. acid potassium phosphate
    C. carbon dioxide   D. glycogen

    3.____

4. Of the following diseases or eruptions, the one which is non-communicable is

    A. ringworm   B. chickenpox
    C. pink eye   D. eczema

    4.____

5. Of the following, the LEAST important in recreation program planning is _____ planning.

    A. hourly   B. daily   C. weekly   D. seasonal

    5.____

6. The area MOST consistently ignored in recreation center programs is

    A. contests and tournaments
    B. hobbies and avocations
    C. family recreation
    D. girls' and women's activities

    6.____

7. Of the following, the instructor's primary duty in preparing a room for an adult discussion group is to

    A. check for proper light, ventilation, and cleanliness
    B. have enough seats for everyone
    C. keep the temperature at 70° Fahrenheit
    D. provide a speaker's table

    7.____

8. The MOST effective procedure for organizing a recreation center council is for the instructor in charge to

    A. call a general meeting of all recreation center members to elect a council
    B. call a meeting of representatives chosen by each of the groups using the center
    C. appoint capable and responsible center members
    D. secure volunteers among center members

    8.____

9. At the first dance of the season, the *No Drinking* rule is violated. Of the following, the BEST procedure is to   9.____

    A. have the police eject the drinkers at the next dance
    B. establish a soft drink bar
    C. discontinue the dances for a month
    D. get the representatives of center organizations to help decide on the action to be taken

10. The BEST single means to be used by the recreation center staff in maintaining continuous and reliable publicity is to   10.____

    A. plan and present occasional special features
    B. maintain a rich, purposeful, well-rounded program
    C. have an effective working relationship with at least one local newspaper sports editor
    D. make and retain the acquaintance of the leaders of the community

11. If a fight between two groups occurs at a recreation center dance, the BEST procedure is to   11.____

    A. break up the fight, let the dance continue, and then investigate the possible causes
    B. notify the police department at once
    C. break up the fight and exclude all participants from the dance
    D. discontinue the dance after stopping the fight

12. Upon discovering a broken window in a crowded gymnasium, you should immediately   12.____

    A. notify the custodian to remove the glass
    B. remove the broken glass from the playing area
    C. ask a member of the center to help you clear the area of glass
    D. try to discover who broke the window

13. As the club coordinator in a newly opened center that has 15 registered clubs, your FIRST step should be to   13.____

    A. tell the clubs you will meet all of them on a specific night
    B. consult the clubs' officers and arrange to meet all of the officers on a specific night
    C. use the bulletin board and other available means to publicize a meeting for all clubs
    D. search out other groups and induce them to form clubs

14. To activate an inactive club council, the BEST procedure is to   14.____

    A. invite well-known speakers to address the group
    B. give added privileges to the club that has the best council attendance
    C. present for solution definite problems that directly affect the welfare of all clubs
    D. have a recreational leader conduct the council for a few weeks

15. The *tip-up* is essentially a stunt that tests   15.____

    A. strength   B. neuro-muscular control
    C. speed   D. balance

16. Success in performing the *headstand* depends primarily on   16.____

    A. forming a triangular base with the hands and the forehead
    B. keeping the knees flexed
    C. moving the legs quickly into position
    D. keeping the fingers spread

17. Of the following stunts, the one which is regarded as the MOST difficult to learn is the   17.____

    A. tip-up   B. headstand
    C. dive and forward roll   D. handstand

18. All of the following are true in the performance of the *duck walk* EXCEPT: 18.____

    A. Fatigue sets in quickly
    B. The feet are separated
    C. A deep knee squatting position is taken
    D. The hips are raised as a forward movement is made

19. *Hand-in* is a term associated with   19.____

    A. volleyball   B. badminton
    C. handball   D. table tennis

20. All of the following terms are associated with badminton EXCEPT   20.____

    A. let   B. rubber   C. set-up   D. hinder

21. In bowling, the term *a turkey* indicates _____ in a row.   21.____

    A. 2 strikes   B. 3 strikes   C. 4 strikes   D. 4 spares

22. Of the following, the prerequisite which is considered most essential for a gymnastic beginner is   22.____

    A. weightlifting   B. tumbling experience
    C. rope climbing ability   D. chin-up ability

23. The term *traveling* is associated with all of the following activities EXCEPT   23.____

    A. basketball   B. the horizontal ladder
    C. the parallel bars   D. volleyball

24. Of the following games, the one which is acknowledged to require the highest degree of neuro-muscular coordination for effective participation is   24.____

    A. volleyball   B. golf
    C. basketball   D. football

25. All of the following terms are associated with basketball EXCEPT   25.____

    A. lay-up   B. post
    C. fault   D. give and go

KEY (CORRECT ANSWERS)

1.	B	11.	A
2.	C	12.	B
3.	D	13.	B
4.	D	14.	C
5.	A	15.	D
6.	C	16.	A
7.	A	17.	D
8.	B	18.	D
9.	D	19.	B
10.	B	20.	D

21.	B
22.	B
23.	D
24.	B
25.	C

TEST 5

DIRECTIONS: Each question or incomplete statement is followed by several suggested answers or completions. Select the one that BEST answers the question or completes the statement. *PRINT THE LETTER OF THE CORRECT ANSWER IN THE SPACE AT THE RIGHT.*

1. *Pyramids* is a term associated with   1.____

   A. trampolining   B. tumbling
   C. side horse   D. parallel bars

2. The term *jump shot* is associated with   2.____

   A. volleyball   B. end ball
   C. basketball   D. putting the shot

3. The number of discs used in the game of shuffleboard is   3.____

   A. four   B. six   C. eight   D. twelve

4. All of the following terms are associated with golf EXCEPT   4.____

   A. hook   B. fade   C. chip   D. let

5. Which of the following games is MOST directly related to basketball?   5.____

   A. Dodge Ball   B. Captain Ball
   C. Call Ball   D. Duck on the Rocks

6. With the first half of a recreation center basketball game ending at 8 o'clock because the teams were not ready on time, and a second game scheduled to start at 8:30 in the same gymnasium, the BEST procedure is to   6.____

   A. hold up the start of the second game until the first game is finished
   B. warn the teams that the first game must end at 8:30
   C. insist that the second half of the first game be played with *running time*
   D. allow the first game to be played until 8:30 and play the remainder of the time at a later date

7. With a recreation center basketball team that is repeatedly 15 minutes late in leaving the building at closing time, the BEST procedure is to   7.____

   A. revoke their permit and give their playing time to another team
   B. make the offenders pay overtime pay for one recreation leader
   C. save time by depriving the team of time for showers
   D. put the team off the court 5 minutes earlier each night until the desired result is achieved

8. With center members who have ignored your warning about possible accidents in the shower room due to *horseplay,* you should   8.____

   A. report offending members to the instructor in charge of the center
   B. stand near the showers while they are in use
   C. permit use of the shower by small groups only
   D. penalize offending members by not allowing them use of the showers for a specified time

9. When you find equipment used by the recreation center in poor condition, the BEST pro-   9.____
cedure is to

    A. leave a note for the recreation supervisor reporting the condition
    B. confer by phone or in person with the center staff
    C. repair the equipment and make no comments so as to maintain friendly relations
    D. restrain staff from using the equipment since the children are probably the offend-
ers

10. To overcome the loss of checkers, chessmen, etc. in a game room, you should   10.____

    A. shorten the length of the game room period to allow time for nightly checking
    B. limit the number of center members in the game room at one time
    C. require a small deposit for the use of a game
    D. require members' signatures on receiving and returning a game

11. While in charge of a game room, you are approached by a number of the recreation cen-   11.____
ter members concerning the addition of new games to the program. You should

    A. refer the member to the instructor in charge of the center
    B. report these requests to the instructor in charge
    C. arrange for fundraising so that new games could be added
    D. make a list of the number and nature of the requests for referral to the instructor in
charge

12. Players of quiet games are disconcerted by the noise made by the players at a table ten-   12.____
nis game in the same room. You should

    A. remind the table tennis players that they are annoying the others
    B. relocate the game areas to avoid interference
    C. explain to the quiet games players that the noise is unintentional
    D. give each type of game a separate time allotment in the program

13. To provide for center members who must at present patiently wait to get a chance to play   13.____
table tennis and hand tennis in a game room, the BEST procedure is to

    A. arrange with the instructor in charge for additional space and equipment for those
games
    B. draw up a time schedule for the members
    C. charge a small fee for each game and buy additional equipment
    D. remove from the game room games that are not as popular

14. You have been assigned to a game room in a recreation center where the ethnic back-   14.____
grounds of the community are predominantly Spanish. In order to establish better rapport, your BEST procedure is to

    A. enlist the aid of an interpreter
    B. learn elementary Spanish
    C. post signs concerning the rules of the game area printed in Spanish
    D. advise members to attend classes for English and citizenship

15. As activity aide assigned to the game room in a recreation center which has a large for-
eign-born membership, you note that some members of the center are gambling on the
outcome of certain games.
Of the following procedures, the BEST one is to

    A. locate the gamblers and revoke their membership cards
    B. post signs in the members' native language telling them gambling is unlawful
    C. maintain constant vigilance so as to prevent rather than detect the gambling
    D. take out of your program those games in which gambling occurs

15.____

16. In order to sustain interest in a recreational program throughout a center season, the
BEST of the following procedures is to

    A. plan the proposed program of activities with and through a committee of the partic-
ipants
    B. post attractive announcements in advance of the opening of each event
    C. invite celebrities in each activity to give talks
    D. have the center award prizes to winners

16.____

17. Upon observing a group of youngsters who show no apparent interest in the center program, you should

    A. anticipate possible interference with other members and politely ask them to leave
    B. be patient and wait until they express a desire to enter an activity
    C. offer them the use of game equipment
    D. discuss with them their reasons for coming to the center

17.____

18. In basketball, the term *discontinued* is associated with

    A. dribbling
    C. the lay-up shot
    B. passing the ball
    D. shooting fouls

18.____

19. Of the following games, the one which is MOST closely related to basketball is

    A. speedball
    C. twenty-one
    B. box ball
    D. center ball

19.____

20. Of the following, which is the LEAST significant factor in determining the game activities
to be offered in a given recreation center program?

    A. Seasonal considerations
    B. Chronological ages
    C. Local interests
    D. Variety as suggested in a text on games

20.____

21. Of the following, the appropriate first aid treatment for heat exhaustion is to

    A. apply cold applications
    B. apply oil
    C. give a drink of cold water
    D. keep patient flat and warm

21.____

22. In administering first aid, the condition that should be treated FIRST is

    A. unconsciousness
    C. fracture of the arm
    B. severe head injury
    D. profuse bleeding

22.____

44

23. The so-called *fuel* foods used by the body are largely made up of   23.____

    A. vitamins   B. fats
    C. proteins   D. carbohydrates

24. The type of wound resulting from a floor burn is known as a(n)   24.____

    A. laceration   B. abrasion
    C. incision   D. puncture

25. Of the following foods, the one generally considered to be richest in minerals is   25.____

    A. fruit   B. pastry   C. cereal   D. meat

KEY (CORRECT ANSWERS)

1.	B	11.	D
2.	C	12.	B
3.	C	13.	B
4.	D	14.	B
5.	B	15.	C
6.	B	16.	A
7.	D	17.	D
8.	D	18.	A
9.	B	19.	C
10.	D	20.	D

21.	D
22.	D
23.	D
24.	B
25.	A

EXAMINATION SECTION
TEST 1

DIRECTIONS: Each question or incomplete statement is followed by several suggested answers or completions. Select the one that BEST answers the question or completes the statement. *PRINT THE LETTER OF THE CORRECT ANSWER IN THE SPACE AT THE RIGHT.*

1. In conducting games for a large group, the instructor should   1.____

   A. correct each mistake made
   B. insist on skilled performance
   C. blow his whistle whenever he sees an infraction of the rules
   D. anticipate blunders by players

2. *Get acquainted* games are of GREATEST value when played in _____ formation.   2.____

   A. file   B. zig-zag   C. circle   D. relay

3. Of the following games, the one MOST closely associated with *Right, left, right, slide and swing* is   3.____

   A. bowling   B. Softball   C. badminton   D. tennis

4. The INCORRECT association is   4.____

   A. cricket - wicket   B. bowling - split
   C. field hockey - crease   D. tennis - advantage

5. The winner of the 2007 Women's United States Open Championship was   5.____

   A. Svetlana Kuznetsova   B. Justine Henin
   C. Maria Sharapova   D. Venus Williams

6. The winner of the 2007 Men's United States Open Championship was   6.____

   A. Roger Federer   B. James Blake
   C. Andy Roddick   D. Novak Djokovic

7. The winner in ice hockey in the 1980 Winter Olympics was   7.____

   A. U.S.S.R.   B. Canada
   C. Great Britain   D. the United States

8. Acclaimed and acknowledged as the greatest professional golfer in history, with tournament prize winnings unequaled by any other player, is   8.____

   A. Jack Nicklaus   B. Tiger Woods
   C. Phil Mickelson   D. Arnold Palmer

9. The only boxer ever to regain the heavyweight championship of the world three times was   9.____

   A. Jack Dempsey
   B. Muhammad Ali (Cassius Clay)
   C. Rocky Marciano
   D. Floyd Patterson

10. In teaching social dancing, the PRIMARY objective of the beginning lesson is to 　　10.___

    A. teach grace and style
    B. create an understanding of the musical background
    C. get the pupil to keep time with the music
    D. teach some fundamental steps so that the pupil can actually dance, regardless of style

11. Of the following, the CHIEF reason why the admission of spectators to athletic competi-　11.___
tions sponsored by the community centers is advisable is that it

    A. makes the activity and its values significant to a large number
    B. provides for greater effort on the part of participants
    C. provides color
    D. helps finance additional activities

12. Of the following, the BEST procedure to follow to prevent the loss of equipment in the 　12.___
community centers is to

    A. mark the equipment with center insignia
    B. place one person in charge of equipment
    C. provide a system for the issuing and accounting of equipment
    D. lecture the members concerning the importance of care of the equipment

13. Of the following, the procedure which is LEAST important in the successful use of a com-　13.___
munity center bulletin board is

    A. limiting notices posted to those that are timely
    B. changing the format used
    C. posting scores
    D. insuring availability of use for posting to all center members

14. A group of relatively inactive middle-aged men join the community center and seek your 　14.___
advice concerning the game best suited for their group.
Which of the following would you recommend?

    A. Basketball   B. Handball   C. Tennis   D. Volleyball

15. Of the following, the MOST important factor in developing good discipline in a physical 　15.___
activities program is

    A. a clearly understood set of rules
    B. a strong instructor personality
    C. an interesting program varied to meet individual interests
    D. prompt treatment of miscreants

16. During the playing of an inter-center basketball game, the spectators demonstrate 　16.___
unsportsmanlike conduct.
The instructor should

    A. recommend that spectators be barred from future games
    B. remove the activity to another gymnasium area apart from spectators and others
    C. stop the game and explain the importance of good sportsmanship on the part of spectators
    D. forfeit the game promptly to the visiting team

17. The community center instructor who observes that a certain high school student is in attendance the five nights a week that the center is open should   17.____

    A. encourage the individual to take full advantage of the athletic program offered
    B. discuss with the student the advisability of such regular attendance
    C. ignore the matter
    D. report the fact to the instructor in charge

18. A group of ten players tends to monopolize a basketball court and, as a consequence, keeps others from playing.   18.____
Of the following, the BEST procedure for the instructor to follow is to

    A. tell these players that they are wrong
    B. establish regulations related to length and frequency and rotation of play
    C. report these ten players to the instructor in charge
    D. insist that these ten players engage in an alternative activity

19. Of the following, the CHIEF advantage of the ladder type of tournament is that it   19.____

    A. provides continuous competition   B. helps the weaker competitor
    C. tends to stabilize competition   D. eliminates the need for handicapping

20. Members of the community centers may be asked to perform all of the following tasks EXCEPT   20.____

    A. opening windows   B. preparing equipment
    C. serving as assistants to the instructor   D. officiating games

21. If many center basketball players miss lay-up shots during games, the BEST procedure for you to follow is to   21.____

    A. correct errors whenever you can
    B. conduct a basketball shooting tournament
    C. show a film on basketball and distribute illustrative material
    D. hold clinics with expert shooters as demonstrators

22. During a basketball game, the scorer's horn sounds while the ball is in play. Following the scorer's horn, a basket is made.   22.____
The referee should rule

    A. no basket   B. violation
    C. basket scores   D. technical foul on home team

23. Of the following, the BEST plan to foster interest in activities other than basketball on the part of center members whose only interest is basketball is to   23.____

    A. discontinue basketball for one week and offer other activities to members
    B. organize beginners' groups in activities other than basketball
    C. require basketball club members to belong to one other club to retain their center membership
    D. arrange for demonstrations by experts in the activities that you wish to promote

24. In volleyball, a legal serve is one in which the ball   24.___

    A. hits the net but goes into the opponent's court
    B. is served with an overhand motion
    C. fails to reach the net
    D. strikes a player on the server's court

25. In volleyball, the player playing in the center at the net is called a   25.___

    A. center back   B. center server
    C. spiker   D. center forward

26. In volleyball, a line ball is   26.___

    A. good   B. a violation
    C. out of bounds   D. played over again

27. In volleyball, the legal method of hitting the ball is   27.___

    A. lifting   B. batting   C. scooping   D. shoving

28. A volleyball authority has suggested that for participants over 40 years of age, the net in   28.___
volleyball should be raised to 8 feet, 6 inches.
The purpose of this proposal is to

    A. eliminate net play
    B. cut down on the number of poor serves
    C. eliminate spiking and call for placement ability
    D. do away with the skill needed for cross-court passing

29. In conducting a demonstration of the skills in volleyball, it is INCORRECT to   29.___

    A. analyze the significant elements in a skill
    B. use skilled players as demonstrators
    C. talk while a skill is being demonstrated
    D. demonstrate a complex technique more than once

30. At the start of a running race, a competitor is in ILLEGAL position if   30.___

    A. his head is in front of the starting line
    B. his hands are on, but not in front of, the starting line
    C. his arm is extended in the air over, but not in front of, the starting line
    D. all parts of his body are behind the starting line

31. Of the following, the FIRST responsibility of the instructor assigned to an activity program   31.___
in a gymnasium is to

    A. see that each person is a participant
    B. provide individual instruction
    C. supervise overall participation to insure safety
    D. insure rotation of participation

32. Participants in the physical activities program of the community center who are not ath-   32._____
letically inclined should be

    A. encouraged to engage in club activities and similar programs that do not require athletic ability
    B. grouped together in simple game programs
    C. urged to limit participation to one physical activity
    D. encouraged to experiment in the expectation that participation in some physical activity will prove satisfying

33. Of the following, the MOST important reason for offering a varied program of athletic   33._____
activities in a community center is to

    A. meet the requirements as outlined by the Division of Community Activities
    B. establish a democratic atmosphere
    C. appeal to varied interests
    D. show a rounded program to the community

34. Of the following, the BEST procedure to follow regarding the conduct of dances in the   34._____
community centers is to

    A. avoid such activities in areas of the city in which racial conflicts may be likely
    B. schedule them once every two weeks
    C. limit them to special feature occasions
    D. have members of the centers plan and conduct these socials

35. Of the following, the factor MOST likely to encourage continued participation of an indi-   35._____
vidual in a particular athletic game activity is

    A. the satisfactions associated with success
    B. comprehensiveness of instruction
    C. the encouragement of the instructor
    D. the approval of peers

36. The activities of an athletic nature selected for a community center program should give   36._____
primary emphasis to

    A. seasonal considerations
    B. the interests of participants
    C. comprehensiveness of opportunities
    D. broadening the interests of participants

37. The FIRST responsibility of the instructor assigned to an evening's activity in the gymna-   37._____
sium is to

    A. prepare materials for group participation
    B. arrange for team participation
    C. inspect the area for potential safety hazards
    D. post the schedule of activities

38. Of the following, the one which BEST explains the thinking of experts in the field of health is that   38.____

   A. all participants over forty years of age should avoid competitive athletic activities
   B. exercise is vital to the well-being of all participants, regardless of age
   C. non-contact sports are to be preferred to contact sports for all participants beyond college age
   D. there is little relationship between exercise and longevity

39. Of the following, the MOST important factor in forming teams for intra-center participation in basketball is   39.____

   A. chronological age   B. similarity of interest
   C. relative skill   D. neighborhood affiliations

40. Of the following team sports, the one which is generally considered MOST popular with participants in the post-adolescent age group is   40.____

   A. volleyball   B. softball   C. punchball   D. soccer

41. The game in which traditionally the opponent is given the benefit of the doubt is   41.____

   A. tennis   B. shuffleboard
   C. volleyball   D. hockey

42. In bowling, the ball should be released   42.____

   A. when the hand starts its upward arc
   B. before the lowest point of the arc has been reached
   C. when the arm is completely extended
   D. when the hand reaches a line parallel to the heel of the forward foot

43. Having a score of 68 in the fifth frame, a bowler scores a strike in the sixth frame, knocks down three pins with his first ball in the seventh frame, and knocks down three pins with his second ball in the seventh frame.
His score at the end of the seventh frame is   43.____

   A. 84   B. 90   C. 94   D. 74

44. Leather goods, such as basketballs and volleyballs, are BEST cleaned by using   44.____

   A. soap and water   B. neats-foot oil
   C. saddle soap   D. brush and water

45. Of the following, the MOST distinctive objective to be especially stressed in the teaching of stunts is to   45.____

   A. develop skill
   B. develop desirable character traits
   C. provide activity interesting to pupils
   D. provide recreational activity

46. Of the following, the one that is indispensable for the enjoyment of MOST forms of recreation is   46.____

   A. expert skill   B. a reasonable degree of efficiency
   C. seriousness of purpose   D. considerable effort

47. The shy or timid individual may be MOST readily recognized by his   47.____

    A. failure to participate in activities
    B. lack of interest in the activities
    C. aimless wandering about the area
    D. lack of skill in playing games

48. Playing two games a night, two nights a week, a round-robin tournament organized for   48.____
nine table-tennis players should last _____ weeks.

    A. 4   B. 9   C. 14   D. 18

49. In conducting an elimination tournament, if the number of entries were 17, the number of   49.____
byes in the first round should be

    A. 1   B. 15   C. 7   D. 5

50. To complete an end of season tournament for four basketball teams in two nights, the   50.____
BEST of the following tournaments is the _____ tournament.

    A. pyramid   B. double elimination
    C. single elimination   D. round-robin

KEY (CORRECT ANSWERS)

1. D	11. A	21. B	31. C	41. A
2. C	12. C	22. C	32. D	42. A
3. A	13. D	23. B	33. C	43. C
4. C	14. D	24. B	34. D	44. C
5. B	15. C	25. D	35. A	45. A
6. A	16. C	26. A	36. B	46. B
7. D	17. B	27. B	37. C	47. A
8. B	18. B	28. A	38. B	48. B
9. B	19. A	29. C	39. C	49. A
10. D	20. A	30. B	40. B	50. C

TEST 2

DIRECTIONS: Each question or incomplete statement is followed by several suggested answers or completions. Select the one that BEST answers the question or completes the statement. *PRINT THE LETTER OF THE CORRECT ANSWER IN THE SPACE AT THE RIGHT.*

1. A tournament in which each player remains in play no matter how many times he wins or loses is called a _____ tournament.

    A. match play   B. double elimination
    C. consolation   D. ladder

1.____

2. Good sportsmanship in intra-center basketball participation is MOST likely to be evidenced if

    A. potentially explosive rivalries are avoided
    B. both teams have discussed sportsmanship in advance of the game
    C. officials and coaches insist on sportsmanlike conduct
    D. penalties are assessed

2.____

3. Good discipline in a community center is usually

    A. the outgrowth of interesting and satisfying participation in activities
    B. the result of a set of rules rigidly enforced
    C. reflective of a strong instructor personality
    D. related to tradition

3.____

4. Of the following activities, the one which is LEAST desirable for the community center program when space is limited and a large number of participants are present is

    A. badminton   B. volleyball
    C. heavy apparatus   D. basketball

4.____

5. Of the following, the LEAST important reason for having student leaders in the physical activity program in the community centers is to

    A. insure safety   B. provide instruction
    C. officiate games   D. promote desirable publicity

5.____

6. The success of clubs in the community center depends for the MOST part on

    A. the number of participants who show an initial interest
    B. the degree of help that the instructor gives the leaders in finding additional members
    C. avoidance of conflict with physical activity programs
    D. the nature of the programs conducted by clubs

6.____

7. Of the following characteristics, the one which is MOST essential to the instructor of physical education is

    A. the ability to perform skills well
    B. an attractive personality
    C. sincerity of purpose
    D. the ability to bring people together

7.____

8. Of the following, the technique LEAST likely to be effective in the teaching of a physical   8.____
   activity skill is

   A. demonstration   B. analysis
   C. explanation   D. practice

9. Of the following, which is the MOST important factor in insuring the success of projected   9.____
   community center programs?

   A. Outlining a long-range program
   B. Involving many participants in the planning process
   C. Posting a complete schedule
   D. Providing advance notice of activities

10. Of the following, the MOST desirable type of leadership of the playground instructor in   10.____
    the conduct of games is that characterized by

    A. continuous participation
    B. lengthy explanation
    C. enforcement of rules
    D. starting games only when each player is thoroughly familiar with its rules

11. Of the following, the one which is considered a PRIME essential in developing an effec-   11.____
    tive club program is

    A. establishing regular meeting schedules
    B. identifying excellent student leadership
    C. providing programs of an interesting nature
    D. rotating the chairmanship

12. Of the following, the factor which is considered LEAST important in insuring a successful   12.____
    club program is

    A. providing for diversified interests
    B. insuring a common interest among a nucleus of participants
    C. publicizing a club schedule
    D. providing interesting programs

13. The rhythmic method of conducting callisthenics is a direct heritage of the _____ sys-   13.____
    tem of gymnastics.

    A. Swedish   B. German   C. English   D. French

14. The health department reports that, of the following, the cause of the GREATEST num-   14.____
    ber of deaths in the city in the past year was

    A. accidents   B. heart disease
    C. cancer   D. diabetes

15. Upon finding a hypodermic needle and a burnt spoon in a hallway of the community cen-   15.____
    ter, you should immediately

    A. close all exits and question everyone in the center
    B. pick up the hypodermic needle and spoon and take them to the custodian
    C. notify the narcotics squad of the police department
    D. pick up the hypodermic needle and spoon and start a search for a person showing
       signs of the use of drugs

16. In the event of an emergency need for an ambulance, we should FIRST call the   16.____

     A. police   B. hospital
     C. health department   D. fire department

17. A direct blow upon a muscle produces a   17.____

     A. sprain   B. fracture   C. contusion   D. strain

18. In the care of a sprained ankle, all of the following procedures are correct EXCEPT   18.____

     A. elevation of the sprained part
     B. application of cold applications
     C. massaging the part to restore circulation
     D. applying a temporary support

19. A person who has fainted should be   19.____

     A. propped up on a pillow or head rest
     B. laid flat and kept quiet
     C. given a warm drink
     D. aroused as soon as possible

20. If, during a community center activity, a person loses consciousness, he is NOT suffering   20.____
from heat exhaustion if his

     A. face is pale   B. pulse is weak
     C. skin is cool and clammy   D. face is flushed

21. In treating heat exhaustion, it is IMPERATIVE that you first   21.____

     A. treat for shock
     B. move the patient to circulating air
     C. keep the body warmly covered
     D. have the patient lie down with head elevated

22. A person during an epileptic seizure should be   22.____

     A. held securely so that he will not struggle
     B. left where he has fallen
     C. carried to the restroom
     D. given a stimulant

23. A sharp-edged instrument would MOST likely cause a(n) _____ wound.   23.____

     A. abrased   B. punctured   C. lacerated   D. incised

24. According to the American Red Cross, carbon monoxide causes death by   24.____

     A. combining more readily with the red blood cells than oxygen does and thus depriv-
ing the body of oxygen
     B. destroying the red blood cells
     C. searing the air sacs of the lungs and preventing oxygen from entering the blood
     D. paralyzing the muscles that function in respiration

25. Of the following, which is the CORRECT statement concerning volleyball? The ball   25.____

    A. must be served underhand
    B. must be struck with an open hand
    C. may be served either underhand or overhand
    D. may be served from any part of the court

26. Which of the following group games does NOT require the use of a ball?   26.____

    A. Bombardment   B. Simon Says
    C. All Run   D. Over and under relay

27. Of the following games, the one which may be played effectively as singles, doubles, or   27.____
with several players on each side is

    A. volleyball   B. deck tennis
    C. badminton   D. handball

28. Of the following games, the one that differs radically from the others in method of scoring   28.____
is

    A. deck tennis   B. badminton
    C. table tennis   D. lawn tennis

29. Which one of the following games does NOT use the term *goal*?   29.____

    A. Hockey   B. Golf   C. Soccer   D. Football

30. In the event of a tie in shuffleboard (doubles), the discs are played   30.____

    A. once from each end
    B. twice from each end
    C. until one team acquires 10 points
    D. as if the game were completely replayed

31. Of the following games, the one which is listed as a tag game is   31.____

    A. two deep   B. dodgeball   C. newcomb   D. end ball

32. Which one of the following is NOT a service *fault* in tennis? The   32.____

    A. serve hits a net post and bounces into the serving box
    B. server steps on the baseline before hitting the ball
    C. server steps on the baseline after hitting the ball
    D. server has both feet off ground before hitting the ball

33. Of the following games, the one which requires the LEAST athletic skill is   33.____

    A. volleyball   B. dodgeball
    C. captain ball   D. shuffleboard

34. The *high lob* shot in tennis is principally used to   34.____

    A. force an opponent to make an unbalanced return shot
    B. drive an opponent back from the net
    C. force an opponent to make a soft return shot
    D. place the ball out of the opponent's reach

35. Of the following, the attribute considered LEAST important in making a good tennis player is   35.____

    A. speed afoot   B. reflexes
    C. size   D. endurance

36. Of the following games, the one which utilizes a circle formation is   36.____

    A. call ball   B. bombardment
    C. stride ball   D. dodgeball

37. Of the following, which exercises will BEST develop balance?   37.____

    A. Head and hand stands   B. Cartwheels
    C. Knee bends   D. Somersaults

38. All of the following represent classification of types of tumbling activities EXCEPT   38.____

    A. rolling   B. balancing   C. springs   D. jumping

39. Of the following, which is the MOST important standard for the tumbler in insuring safe participation?   39.____

    A. Participating in tumbling only when properly costumed
    B. Attempting only stunts which are within his own ability
    C. Participating in tumbling only when mats are clean and in good repair
    D. Lifting only individuals who are lighter in weight than himself

40. To develop in clubs a sense of responsibility for the conduct of visitors at a basketball game, the BEST procedure is to   40.____

    A. require a damage deposit from the clubs
    B. charge admission to the game
    C. require the club to provide funds for additional instructors
    D. hold the clubs responsible for the conduct of the visitors

41. To stimulate greater interest in a game room that offers checkers, chess, nok-hockey, dominoes, and table tennis, the BEST procedure is to   41.____

    A. increase the number of games offered
    B. use the bulletin board to advertise the location of the game room
    C. start a ladder tournament for each game offered
    D. invite club participation by giving clubs exclusive use of the room at specific times

42. Parents have been forbidding their children to frequent the center because of ugly rumors they have heard.
To meet this situation, the BEST procedure is to   42.____

    A. publicly challenge anyone to prove the rumors
    B. call a meeting of a representative community group to openly discuss the situation
    C. determine who is responsible and have him deny the rumor
    D. bring the matter to the attention of your supervisors and have the Board of Education investigate

43. Upon discovering two members of the center smoking cigarettes on a stairway, you should

    43.____

    A. take them to an exit and make certain they leave the building
    B. tell them to put out the lighted cigarette and, in the future, to step outside the building to smoke
    C. warn them that smoking is forbidden and they are liable to arrest
    D. tell them to put out the lighted cigarette, take their membership cards, and exclude them for the night

44. The MOST comprehensive objective of the community center is to provide opportunity for

    44.____

    A. the development of athletic skills
    B. social and cultural interaction among the members of the community
    C. the members of the community to receive instruction in a variety of recreational skills
    D. trained personnel to create a wholesome recreational area in which to combat juvenile delinquency

45. The MAIN job in a community center public relations program is to

    45.____

    A. obtain publicity for tournament activities
    B. maintain rapport with local newspapers
    C. develop sensitivity to the needs and desires of the community
    D. make the center's facilities available to all organized groups in the community

46. Of the following, the LEAST effective method of expanding the co-educational program of a center is to

    46.____

    A. have the center council plan a center-wide dance
    B. organize a forum for the discussion of teenage problems
    C. conduct a girls' basketball tournament
    D. introduce such activities as mixed badminton, shuffle-board, and table tennis

47. In order to encourage participation by girls in the community center program, the BEST of the following activities is a

    47.____

    A. girls' table tennis tournament with suitable prizes
    B. coed canteen with dancing
    C. charm course given with the aid of a cosmetics company
    D. coed volleyball game

48. Of the following, the MOST desirable method of curbing vandalism committed by some community center members is to

    48.____

    A. assign enough instructors to patrol the building
    B. make the center members conscious of their responsibility for bettering the situation
    C. request assistance from the local Police Athletic League officer
    D. use one centrally located area for all activities

49. In a community center gymnasium, some members are not dressed in shorts and gym shirts.
    The instructor assigned to this area should

    A. tell the members to dress uniformly
    B. tactfully explain to the members the values of uniform appearance
    C. say nothing to the members concerning their dress
    D. warn them once, and if they fail to dress uniformly, report them to the person in charge of the center

49.____

50. In anticipation of delays and interruptions due to mechanical difficulties during an auditorium program of movies, you should plan to

    A. deliver a talk about the center program
    B. conduct a community sing
    C. conduct a campaign for a second projector
    D. ask volunteers in the audience to entertain

50.____

KEY (CORRECT ANSWERS)

1. D	11. C	21. B	31. A	41. C
2. C	12. C	22. B	32. C	42. B
3. A	13. B	23. D	33. D	43. B
4. A	14. A	24. A	34. B	44. B
5. D	15. C	25. C	35. C	45. C
6. D	16. A	26. B	36. D	46. C
7. C	17. C	27. B	37. A	47. B
8. C	18. C	28. D	38. D	48. B
9. B	19. B	29. B	39. B	49. B
10. A	20. D	30. B	40. D	50. B

TEST 3

DIRECTIONS: Each question or incomplete statement is followed by several suggested answers or completions. Select the one that BEST answers the question or completes the statement. *PRINT THE LETTER OF THE CORRECT ANSWER IN THE SPACE AT THE RIGHT.*

1. Upon discovering that a community center member has intentionally damaged school property, the BEST procedure is to

   A. take his membership card and expel him
   B. deny him admission to the center until he pays for the damage
   C. turn the matter over to the custodian
   D. hold him until the police arrive

   1.____

2. In spite of an earlier promise to desist, a boy opens the rear doors of the center to allow non-members to enter the center.
   You should

   A. take his membership card and expel him from the center
   B. make him a member of the center council to develop a sense of civic responsibility
   C. warn him that you are going to watch him closely
   D. suspend him until he brings a parent to see you

   2.____

3. When factions of the center membership get into a situation that threatens to develop into a gang war, the BEST of the following procedures is to

   A. notify the local police station at once
   B. refer the matter to the center council for consideration at the next meeting
   C. tell the boys that unless they cooperate with you, they will be expelled
   D. attempt to resolve their differences through personal mediation

   3.____

4. During an argument in a community center, a boy is superficially cut by a knife.
   After treating the wound, you should

   A. take the boys into the office to settle their differences
   B. hold those involved and call the police
   C. send for the parents of the offender and turn the matter over to them
   D. get the names and addresses of the two boys involved and send a complete report to the day school principal

   4.____

5. Of the following, the BEST procedure for getting an initial *in* with a local street gang is to

   A. make contact with the gang at a place like a candy store where the gang gathers
   B. offer the gang the use of center facilities
   C. get the favor of one of the members of the gang and be introduced to the leader
   D. form a club for the gang and sponsor its membership in the center council

   5.____

6. In which of the following games are the services of an official LEAST essential?

   A. Softball   B. Golf   C. Tennis   D. Soccer

   6.____

7. All of the following terms are associated with volleyball EXCEPT

   A. set-up   B. attack   C. block   D. slam

   7.____

8. The term *fault*, to indicate an error, is used in each of the following sports EXCEPT   8._____

   A. tennis   B. bowling   C. handball   D. badminton

9. The term *spot bowling* is a reference to   9._____

   A. strategic placing of a bowler in the team's lineup
   B. aiming at one particular pin during delivery
   C. aiming at a particular spot on the alley during delivery
   D. use of a substitute bowler as a team fill-in

10. Of the following, the BEST method of teaching skills in basketball is   10._____

    A. to give longer drill periods to increase concentration
    B. through incidental learning
    C. to give intensive lectures with a blackboard
    D. to give short periods of practice with frequent changes

11. Of the following types of basketball passes, the one which is considered the MOST accu-   11._____
    rate is the _____ pass.

    A. two-hand overhead   B. blind
    C. one-hand bounce   D. baseball

12. Of the following, the rule concerning a free throw in basketball is that   12._____

    A. the shooter has ten seconds to attempt the shot
    B. the shooter may take a *reasonable* period of time before attempting the throw
    C. no time limit is imposed
    D. the shooter may make his attempt not more than five seconds after approaching
       the foul line

13. Of the following elements of basketball, which has changed MOST radically in the last   13._____
    twenty-five years?

    A. Dribbling the ball   B. Techniques in guarding
    C. Methods of passing   D. Techniques in shooting

14. In teaching beginners the game of basketball, of the following, the BEST procedure for   14._____
    the instructor to follow is to

    A. organize teams promptly
    B. limit participation to the practice of skills taught
    C. organize participation in games that use the skills that have been taught
    D. teach all the fundamental skills individually

15. All of the following are effective cues in catching a basketball thrown chest height or   15._____
    higher EXCEPT

    A. point the fingers up
    B. keep the thumbs back
    C. keep the hands well behind the ball
    D. keep the arms well back

16. If basketball is a major activity in the community center gymnasium to which you are assigned, it would be advisable to

    A. seek knowledgeable members to referee games
    B. referee games yourself
    C. arrange to hire experienced referees
    D. have each team provide a referee from among its team members

16.____

17. Of the following, the one which represents the BEST sequence of skills for instructional purposes when teaching basketball to beginners is

    A. foul shooting, dribbling, lay-up shot
    B. dribbling, lay-up shot, passing
    C. dribbling, passing, lay-up shot
    D. passing, lay-up shot, dribbling

17.____

18. When a boy who looks younger than high school age produces a general organization card from a nearby high school while attempting to enroll as a center member, you should

    A. enroll him but reserve the right to recall his membership card
    B. take the general organization card and expel him
    C. question the center members about the situation
    D. question him about the names of his instructors, the courses he is taking, and general high school procedures

18.____

19. When placed in charge of the auditorium for the first lecture on community problems to be followed by questions from the audience, your MOST important job is to

    A. provide for a speaker's table and chairs
    B. check the heat and lighting arrangements
    C. be alert in supervision so that interference with the speaker will not happen
    D. open the meeting, explain what is expected of the audience, and ask for complete audience cooperation

19.____

20. To get the attention of the entire group when you blow a whistle in a community center gymnasium, you should

    A. adopt a *get tough* attitude
    B. gently chide the entire group for inattention
    C. have individual talks with those that do not respond
    D. make the second blast of the whistle louder than the first

20.____

21. Your basketball team of center A is scheduled to play at center B. You should

    A. arrange to meet your team at center B a half hour before game time
    B. meet your team at center A, give explicit directions for reaching center B, and proceed independently
    C. accompany your team from center A to center B
    D. arrange to meet at one transportation point and proceed to center B

21.____

22. During a basketball game, the spectator members of your center disconcert visiting play-   22.____
    ers while shooting fouls.
    You should

    A.   immediately eject the offenders
    B.   move about the area and tell the members to be more courteous
    C.   stop the game and request the spectators to stop their actions
    D.   stop the game and award the game to the visitors

23. In your center, a major portion of gymnasium space and time is allotted to organized   23.____
    teams but a large group of teenagers engage in unorganized scrimmage when the
    courts are free.
    Of the following procedures, the BEST one is to

    A.   organize the teenagers into clubs and allot them playing time
    B.   allow more time for free play
    C.   ask each organized team to solicit new members
    D.   organize a one basket, three-man round robin tournament for the teenagers

24. Upon your arrival at the community center twenty minutes before the center opens, you   24.____
    find a group of ten boys waiting to get in.
    You should

    A.   allow them to enter and use the basement facilities
    B.   organize them into a squad to help set up the equipment
    C.   keep them outside until the center opens
    D.   permit them to enter but tell them that in the future they must wait until opening
         time

25. When you observe a person making several attempts to open a combination lock on a   25.____
    locker, you should

    A.   suspect that he is not the rightful owner and question him
    B.   wait until he has opened the lock and then question him about the contents
    C.   personally offer to help open the lock
    D.   tell another center member to help the person

_____

KEY (CORRECT ANSWERS)

1. B	11. A
2. D	12. A
3. B	13. D
4. A	14. C
5. C	15. D
6. B	16. A
7. D	17. C
8. B	18. D
9. C	19. D
10. D	20. C

21. C
22. B
23. A
24. B
25. C

———

EXAMINATION SECTION
TEST 1

DIRECTIONS: Each question or incomplete statement is followed by several suggested answers or completions. Select the one that BEST answers the question or completes the statement. *PRINT THE LETTER OF THE CORRECT ANSWER IN THE SPACE AT THE RIGHT.*

1. In a playground, when a group fails repeatedly to respond to the teacher's command, the BEST procedure for the teacher to follow, of the following, is to   1.____

    A. reprimand the group in an adequate voice that commands attention
    B. single out the worst offenders for punishment
    C. consult the teacher in charge
    D. provide a period of inactivity until attention is given by all

2. Of the following, the MOST important characteristic of children's discipline in the playground is that discipline   2.____

    A. results from habitual response
    B. is self-imposed
    C. is automatic when requested by the teacher
    D. grows out of respect for the teacher

3. Of the following functions of the teacher assigned to the game room in a playground, the one which is LEAST significant is   3.____

    A. assigning activities to specific areas
    B. insuring rotational participation
    C. instructing student leaders
    D. supervising personally to insure against loss of equipment

4. Of the following, the MOST important consideration in organizing groups for active games is   4.____

    A. chronological age
    B. previous knowledge of the game
    C. recency of participation
    D. strenuousness of the activity

5. Of the following statements concerning the inclusion of individual and group activities in a playground program, the one MOST sound educationally is: 5.____

    A. Group activities should be used exclusively so as to give stress to social values and outcomes
    B. Individual and group activities should be included and equal emphasis given to each
    C. Individual activities should be included only when children request them
    D. Individual activities should be included but greater emphasis should be placed on group activities

6. Of the following, the practice which is LEAST important in making effective use of bulletin boards in playgrounds is: 6.____

A. Displays should be changed frequently
B. Emphasis should be given to student participation in the preparation of displays
C. Displays should be artistically attractive
D. All notices should be illustrated when possible

7. Of the following age groups, the one which is generally MOST vitally interested in games that entail team play is   7.____

    A. six to eight   B. eight to ten
    C. ten to twelve   D. twelve to fourteen

8. Of the following, the one which is LEAST desirable as a daily activity in the vacation play-grounds is   8.____

    A. several group games   B. a team game
    C. a quiet game period   D. a calisthenics period

9. The use of a whistle in the playground should be   9.____

    A. limited to getting the attention of a group
    B. employed as a means of drawing attention to a phase of the program
    C. used only at the beginning of the day to start the program
    D. restricted to a soft, warbling sound

10. During the play period in a crowded play area, the teacher's prime responsibility is to   10.____

    A. provide instructional assistance for individual pupils
    B. see that all students participate
    C. supervise so as to insure safe participation
    D. rotate activities fairly

11. All of the following are essential to a successful playground program EXCEPT   11.____

    A. plans for rainy day activities
    B. *quiet* activities
    C. individual competitions
    D. group activities

12. Of the following statements, the one which constitutes the BEST reason for developing a playground newspaper is: 12.____

    A. Information can be readily transmitted by parents and students
    B. Vocational interests may be awakened
    C. An additional activity of interest to some students is provided
    D. The reputation of the playground is enhanced

13. Of the following, the BEST way to gain new participants in the playground program is to   13.____

    A. advertise through placards in neighborhood stores
    B. write to parents about the program
    C. provide a program interesting to all age groups
    D. provide prizes for competition

14. All of the following statements concerning bowling are true EXCEPT: 14.____

A.   The straight ball is harder to control than the hooked ball
B.   The hooked ball delivery is a more efficient pin-getter than the straight ball delivery
C.   The ball should be aimed at the 1-3 pocket by right-handed bowlers
D.   A hooked delivery is effected by turning the wrist and forearm as the ball is released

15.   The President, concerned by the problem of physical fitness, has recommended   15._____

A.   an expansion of the intramural and varsity athletic programs
B.   a return to formal calisthenics
C.   fifteen minutes of daily physical activity for all normal boy and girl students
D.   an emphasis on walking

16.   All of the following statements about the selection of activities constituting the playground   16._____
program are true EXCEPT:

A.   Children should participate in selecting a program of activities
B.   The program should be varied and include quiet activities
C.   An exact plan for each day should be arranged at least a week in advance
D.   Programs can best be evaluated by teachers and pupils cooperatively

17.   All of the following statements concerning leadership among children of playground age   17._____
are true EXCEPT:

A.   All children openly aspire to be leaders
B.   Leadership should be encouraged through adequate opportunity
C.   Most often leadership should be related to individual activities rather than general-
ized
D.   Group participation in the selection of leaders is essential

18.   Of the following, the objective which should be given PRIMARY emphasis in an athletic   18._____
tournament program in a playground is

A.   extensive participation
B.   identification and recognition of winners
C.   the learning of specific athletic skills
D.   learning how to lose

19.   The teacher should conduct an inspection of the play area to which he is assigned prior   19._____
to the start of the activities PRIMARILY to

A.   insure that sufficient equipment is available
B.   insure safe participation
C.   be able to report conditions or situations to the responsible person in charge
D.   check the inventory of equipment

20.   Of the following, the one which is the MOST persistent problem in the average vacation   20._____
playground is

A.   identifying games of interest to the participants
B.   encouraging pupils to participate
C.   gaining parental cooperation
D.   providing significant athletic participation for large numbers simultaneously

21. If a fist fight occurs between two students in the playground, of the following, the BEST   21.____
    way to handle the situation is to

    A. send for the parents of each combatant
    B. punish both summarily
    C. insist that each explain his feelings and his reasons for fighting to the other
    D. demand an apology from each when the fight is stopped

22. The relative placement of activities in a play area should be determined PRIMARILY by   22.____

    A. the size of the area
    B. the popularity of the activities
    C. the wishes of participants
    D. safety factors

23. Of the following statements, the one which BEST expresses a sound philosophy con-   23.____
    cerning assembly programs is:

    A. Assembly programs should always be educational rather than a source of enter-
        tainment
    B. Assembly programs should be held at stated intervals without variation
    C. Assembly programs should be held only when a significant purpose is to be served
    D. All students attending the playground should attend each assembly unless the
        number of students involved makes this impossible

24. Of the following, the one which represents the BEST method of grouping displays for an   24.____
    art and hobby show is

    A. relative ages of the participants and the types of exhibit
    B. types of exhibit only
    C. degrees of excellence
    D. random placement

25. Regarding trips sponsored by the playground, all of the following statements are correct   25.____
    EXCEPT:

    A. Trips planned for children in the vacation playground should always be planned to
        achieve cultural values
    B. Success of a trip depends to a large degree on the teacher's prior knowledge of
        opportunities and advisable details
    C. Trips may be scheduled as a reward for effective participation in the playground
        program
    D. Parents should be encouraged to assist in conducting trips

26. All of the following are true of the game *Circle Stride Ball* EXCEPT: 26.____

    A. The ball is kicked by the player who is *It*
    B. A basketball is used
    C. Players in the circle place hands on knees until the ball is in play
    D. *Feinting* by the one who is *It* is very helpful

27. Of the following, the practice regarding monitors which is NOT justifiable is   27.____

    A. giving student monitors an award for service at the end of the season
    B. selecting students as monitors who want to serve
    C. keeping student monitors out of tournament competitions
    D. using the older children as monitors

28. Of the following, the LEAST reliable indicator of the extent to which pupils enjoy the play-   28.____
ground program generally is

    A. the infrequency or absence of vandalism
    B. the extent of participation in any given tournament
    C. attendance in general
    D. opinions of parents and others

29. Of the following qualities or considerations, the one which is MOST important in the   29.____
selection of student monitors is

    A. skill in performing the given service
    B. leadership potential endorsed by peer approval
    C. previous experience
    D. desire to perform the service

30. All of the following statements concerning the game *Three Deep* are true EXCEPT: 30.____

    A. *Three Deep* is a variation of *Two Deep*
    B. *Three Deep* can be played as a circle or as a line game
    C. One runner and one chaser are used in *Three Deep*
    D. *Three Deep* has general appeal to all age groups coming to the playground

31. Of the following, the procedure which is LEAST important in insuring the success of a *tal-*   31.____
ent show is

    A. previewing the *talent* available
    B. adequately advertising the event through advance notice
    C. selecting an appropriate time for the show
    D. limiting the number of performers to those few who demonstrate exceptional talent

32. Of the following, the one which constitutes the LEAST justifiable reason for taking a   32.____
group of students to a professional baseball game is that

    A. it is an opportunity for cooperative planning
    B. it tends to broaden interests in recreational opportunities
    C. it provides an opportunity for parents to cooperate as chaperons
    D. social skills and graces may be encouraged and developed

33. Of the following statements, the one which represents the SOUNDEST point of view con-   33.____
cerning the participation of handicapped students in the vacation playground program is:

    A. Severely handicapped children should be discouraged from attending
    B. Activities provided for them should approximate those planned for the normal and
       provide adaptations consistent with their handicaps

C. Handicapped children should be segregated from the normal children for all athletic activities

D. Handicapped children should be encouraged to participate in quiet games and avoid activities of an active nature

34. All of the following procedures are desirable in effecting the success of an *art and hobby* show in the playground EXCEPT: 34.____

    A. Showing should be limited to those items which meet a predetermined standard of excellence

    B. Such an activity should be scheduled for late in the playground season

    C. Publicity should be planned so as to insure having visitors

    D. Pupils should actively participate in planning the show

35. Of the following qualities or abilities, the one which is LEAST necessary in playing the game *Snatch the Club* is   35.____

    A. speed afoot   B. quick reflexes

    C. strength   D. good balance

36. Of the following athletic activities, the one which is BEST suited to the interests of nine and ten year old boys is   36.____

    A. basketball   B. dodgeball

    C. badminton   D. captain ball

37. Of the following phases of planning, the one in which the participation of children may be MOST effective is in   37.____

    A. selecting activities and determining their sequence

    B. determining expected outcomes

    C. establishing safety rules

    D. deciding on best use of space

38. Of the following, the MOST important factor in determining the activities to be included in a successful program is   38.____

    A. an analysis of activities generally successful in all other playgrounds

    B. the particular interests displayed by the students served in a given playground

    C. the relative importance of activities as revealed by standard texts on group games and activities

    D. the opinion of teachers assigned to a given playground

39. All of the following statements concerning the game *Line Zig Zag* are true EXCEPT: 39.____

    A. Only one basketball or volleyball for each team can be used

    B. Variations in formations are desirable

    C. Accurate running is unnecessary

    D. Skill in throwing and catching is stressed

40. Of the following procedures, on the part of the teacher, the one which is MOST likely to cause poor discipline is   40.____

    A. punishing infractions too severely

    B. threatening disciplinary action and failing to carry out the punishment

C. failing to identify the true peer leadership among students
D. being impatient with children

41. Of the following, the BEST method of developing self-discipline in a child is to

    A. have the teacher explain the necesssity for it
    B. associate self-discipline with peer sanctions
    C. provide punishment for breaches of discipline
    D. involve the parents when need for discipline develops

41._____

42. Of the following, the one which is LEAST important as a safety factor in the playing of dodgeball is the

    A. size of the circle
    B. adherence to the rules
    C. strength of the players
    D. size of the basketball or volleyball used

42._____

43. Of the following, the BEST way to motivate children in playing a group game new to them is to provide

    A. a complete explanation of the rules and regulations before starting to play
    B. a detailed explanation of the rules accompanied by several demonstrations
    C. minimal rules and explanations before starting the play
    D. practice in skills needed in the playing of the game

43._____

44. All of the following statements concerning the showing of movies in a playground are true EXCEPT:

    A. The teacher should preview a movie
    B. Movies should always have educational as well as entertainment values
    C. Movies should be shown on rainy days rather than on a regular schedule
    D. Children should play a part in selecting movies

44._____

45. Of the following, the one which is the LEAST important in developing specific athletic skills is

    A. analysis of the skill
    B. demonstration of the skill or skills
    C. individual corrections
    D. posters demonstrating sequential movements

45._____

46. Of the following statements, the one which constitutes the MOST desirable statement concerning the officiating of team games in the playground is:

    A. The teacher should officiate regularly to insure accuracy and impartiality
    B. Children should be trained as quickly as possible to act as officials
    C. A few capable older students should be used exclusively as officials
    D. The teacher should never serve as an official

46._____

47. All of the following are true of the game of Bombardment EXCEPT:

    A. Indian clubs are used
    B. The object is to strike an opponent

47._____

C. The area of play is divided into equal halves
D. Players may not step over the center line

48. In the playground, the MOST important criterion, of the following, concerning the scheduling of puppetry is that   48.____

    A. every child has an exploratory opportunity to develop an interest in it
    B. only students skilled in it are encouraged to continue
    C. it may be substituted for more strenuous activities
    D. its entertainment values are stressed

49. Of the following sport skills, the one in which the action of the feet is LEAST important is   49.____

    A. pitching a baseball
    B. hitting a golf ball
    C. shooting a foul in basketball
    D. putting the shot

50. In basketball, when a ball gets stuck in a basket support, the official should   50.____

    A. give the ball to the team whose member touched it last
    B. call a jump ball
    C. award the ball to the team defending against the attempted shot
    D. allow possession to the team that dislodges the ball

51. Of the following values or outcomes of group games conducted in the playground, the one which is of PRIME value is   51.____

    A. skill in playing the game
    B. detailed understanding of the rules of play
    C. lasting recreational skills
    D. social skills and graces

52. Badminton is similar to tennis in all of the following respects EXCEPT: 52.____

    A. Both games lend themselves to *doubles* play
    B. Serving is similar
    C. Courts are changed similarly
    D. The term *let* is used in both games

53. Of the following, the activity associated with the game *Prisoner's Base* is   53.____

    A. throwing a ball   B. tagging an opponent
    C. hiding and seeking   D. identifying names

54. All of the following are correct statements about the game *Squirrels in Trees* EXCEPT: 54.____

    A. When large numbers participate, a tree is represented by two players who join hands
    B. An extra *squirrel* without a tree is needed
    C. *Squirrels* change *trees* simultaneously
    D. Circles may be used for trees when numbers are small

55. All of the following concerning badminton are correct EXCEPT: 55._____

    A. A men's single game consists of fifteen or twenty-one points
    B. The top of the net at the posts should measure slightly more than five feet above the floor
    C. In doubles each player on the side winning the toss has a chance to serve in the first inning
    D. The players shall serve from and receive service in their respective right-hand courts only when the server's score is zero or when he has scored an even number of points

56. In teaching young children the game of tennis, the teacher's PRIMARY objective should   56._____
be to

    A. develop ability to plan and execute strategic games
    B. teach fundamentals
    C. enrich leisure time
    D. develop and cultivate interest

57. The *volley* in tennis, by definition, is a   57._____

    A. rapid interchange
    B. consecutive series of forehand shots
    C. series of shots that barely clear the net
    D. series of shots during which the ball does not hit the ground

58. All of the following are correct cues in the teaching of tennis EXCEPT: 58._____

    A. Keep the body weight on the balls of the feet
    B. Flex the knees in preparation for a shift to a backhand or forehand position
    C. Move the right foot forward on a forehand drive, if right-handed
    D. Play an open stance on cross-court passing shots

59. Of the following games, the one which BEST lends itself to various forms or adaptations   59._____
of play is

    A. dodgeball   B. end ball
    C. captain ball   D. corner ball

60. All of the following concerning volleyball are true statements EXCEPT: 60._____

    A. An official team consists of eight players
    B. Both feet must be placed behind the service line in making the serve
    C. A maximum of three passes is permitted before returning the ball
    D. Only the serving team scores points

61. *Jump the Shot* is a game that essentially requires   61._____

    A. quick response
    B. ability to handle a rope in lasso fashion
    C. strength to *put the shot*
    D. accuracy in throwing

62. Of the following, the game which MOST NEARLY resembles *End Ball* is
    62.____

    A. basketball   B. dodgeball
    C. circle stride ball   D. captain ball

63. Overhead and underleg relay races are PRIMARILY of value in that they
    63.____

    A. provide for the practice of basketball skills
    B. afford opportunity to large numbers of participants to enjoy the activity
    C. offer a field in which only simple skills are needed
    D. appeal to any age group

64. Of the following games, the one which employs circles and Indian clubs is
    64.____

    A. Snatch the Bacon   B. Blind Man's Bluff
    C. All Up Relay   D. Bull in the Ring

65. All of the following are true of the game *Numbers Change* EXCEPT:
    65.____

    A. It may be played on a playground or in a classroom
    B. It may be played as a tag game
    C. A line formation rather than a circle is usually used
    D. All the players beginning with the center players count off in threes

66. All of the following are true of *Indian Leg Wrestling* EXCEPT:
    66.____

    A. Combatants assume a supine position
    B. Several *counts* precede actual wrestling
    C. Timing is as important as strength
    D. Injuries easily result in this activity

67. In order to complete a single round robin tournament for six teams, the number of games that MUST be scheduled is
    67.____

    A. 9   B. 12   C. 15   D. 18

68. All of the following are well-established types of tournament EXCEPT
    68.____

    A. elimination   B. ladder
    C. round robin   D. progressive

69. In planning a four day table tennis tournament for eleven players, in which no player will compete in more than one match a day, the number of byes necessary in the first round will be
    69.____

    A. two   B. three   C. four   D. five

70. The game *Going to Jerusalem* is also known as
    70.____

    A. musical chairs   B. Simon wants
    C. round the bases   D. highway tag

71. Of the following, the one which represents the BEST number of players to engage in a game of *Snatch the Club* is
    71.____

    A. six   B. eight   C. twenty   D. thirty

72. All of the following are true of the game of *Nok Hockey* EXCEPT: 72._____
    A. It is essentially a game for two players
    B. Good reflexes are helpful in playing this game
    C. The successful playing of the game requires skill comparable to that employed in table tennis
    D. *Nok Hockey* is popular with both boys and girls

73. All of the following associations are correct EXCEPT   73._____
    A. Indian wrestle - individual combative activity
    B. Three Deep - line game
    C. Newcomb - variation of volleyball
    D. trampoline - heavy apparatus

74. All of the following are considered games of low organization EXCEPT   74._____
    A. dodgeball   B. handball
    C. end ball   D. captain ball

75. It is generally conceded that posters concerning safety activities and the like for use in   75._____
    the playground are MOST effective when
    A. made professionally
    B. made professionally and illustrated with cartoons
    C. prepared on varied colored backgrounds
    D. conceived and made by the children themselves

KEY (CORRECT ANSWERS)

1.	D	16.	C	31.	D	46.	B	61.	A
2.	B	17.	A	32.	C	47.	B	62.	D
3.	D	18.	A	33.	B	48.	A	63.	B
4.	A	19.	B	34.	A	49.	C	64.	C
5.	D	20.	D	35.	C	50.	B	65.	C
6.	D	21.	C	36.	B	51.	D	66.	D
7.	D	22.	D	37.	A	52.	B	67.	C
8.	D	23.	C	38.	B	53.	B	68.	D
9.	A	24.	A	39.	A	54.	A	69.	D
10.	C	25.	A	40.	B	55.	C	70.	A
11.	C	26.	A	41.	B	56.	D	71.	C
12.	C	27.	C	42.	D	57.	D	72.	C
13.	C	28.	B	43.	C	58.	C	73.	B
14.	A	29.	B	44.	B	59.	A	74.	B
15.	C	30.	B	45.	D	60.	A	75.	D

TEST 2

DIRECTIONS: Each question or incomplete statement is followed by several suggested answers or completions. Select the one that BEST answers the question or completes the statement. *PRINT THE LETTER OF THE CORRECT ANSWER IN THE SPACE AT THE RIGHT.*

1. Of the following, the practice MOST likely to promote good discipline in a playground is the   1.____

   A. establishment of definite rules and punishments for their violation
   B. scheduling of an interesting program of activities
   C. establishment of effective relationships with parents
   D. assignment of student assistants

2. All of the following are true of the game *Maze Tag* EXCEPT: 2.____

   A. All but two players stand in parallel lines or ranks with hands clasped
   B. The success of the game depends on the judgment of the leader in giving commands
   C. It is a foul to tag across clasped hands
   D. This game is suited to a maximum of forty players

3. In a playground, *Play Day* programs are intended PRIMARILY to   3.____

   A. substitute for inter-playground tournaments
   B. provide opportunities for the skilled performers to demonstrate their abilities
   C. provide girls with competitive opportunities
   D. encourage the less able athletically as well as others to participate

4. All of the following concerning the game *Captain Ball* are true EXCEPT: 4.____

   A. Players are assigned to one or the other half of the court
   B. A series of small circles, drawn on the floor, is used
   C. The object of the game is to score as many *baskets* as possible in a given period of time
   D. Passing the ball is stressed

5. All of the following statements concerning the interests of boys and girls in sports activities are true EXCEPT: 5.____

   A. Chronological age groupings of participants are not of major importance
   B. Activities selected by students are influenced by seasonal considerations
   C. Experiential backgrounds are important determinants of interest
   D. Pre-teenagers generally have a high degree of interest in group games

6. Of the following, the method recommended for teaching the dribble in basketball to beginners is to   6.____

   A. have them participate in the game itself
   B. organize relays employing dribbling
   C. have students practice individually until success is achieved
   D. practice dribbling in conjunction with other skills

78

7. In tennis, a ball that touches the net and then drops in the service area on service is referred to as a 7._____

    A. let ball   B. fault   C. foul ball   D. net ball

8. *Squat Tug* is a stunt in which 8._____

    A. an eight-foot rope is used
    B. one opponent joins hands with the other
    C. more than two contestants participate
    D. pushing is permitted

9. All of the following concerning shuffleboard are true EXCEPT: 9._____

    A. Hesitation or hook shots are permissible
    B. A disc or discs returning or remaining on the court after having struck any object other than a live disc shall be removed before further play
    C. A disc which stops in the area between the farthest dead line and the starting area is dead and shall be removed before further play
    D. A disc which is more than halfway over the side of the court and which rests or leans on the edge shall be immediately removed

10. On an official volleyball court with ample space beyond the end lines, the serving area is located 10._____

    A. within the court to the right of the center of the end line
    B. in an area six feet deep back of the end line and between the extensions of the side lines
    C. across the back of the entire court between the end line and a parallel line 3 feet from it
    D. any place beyond the end line

11. Of the following, the one which would be the MOST suitable preliminary activity for a *play day* program is 11._____

    A. a treasure hunt   B. a softball game
    C. quiet games   D. calisthenics

12. Referees who are peers of students in the playground experience their GREATEST difficulty in gaining 12._____

    A. agreement on the interpretation of rules
    B. acceptance in matters where judgment is required
    C. respect for the official as a nonpartisan
    D. respect for the experience of the official

13. The material needed to play the game *box ball* is a 13._____

    A. series of squares   B. basketball
    C. handball   D. small racket

14. A right-handed bowler in an elementary skills group should be taught to direct the ball so that it makes contact between pins 14._____

    A. one and two   B. seven and ten
    C. one and three   D. nine and ten

15. All of the following statements regarding the game of shuffleboard are correct EXCEPT: 15.____

    A. Players may leave the court without permission
    B. Play continues until all discs have been shot even if game point has been reached
    C. In singles, one round of play shall decide a tie
    D. In doubles, any remark or motion to partner which indicates coaching his play is prohibited

16. All of the following concerning the development of dramatic activities in the playground   16.____
program are true EXCEPT:

    A. The play chosen must be suited to the understanding of the age group
    B. The teacher should establish the interpretation for the children
    C. The teacher should allow other children to watch certain rehearsals
    D. Extra characters may be created to broaden participation

17. Of the following, the statement that indicates the LEAST important determinant in the   17.____
selection of student leaders in the playground is:

    A. Only the older children should be eligible
    B. Selection for various posts of leadership should be determined by ability and inter-
est
    C. Student leaders chosen should have peer approval
    D. Objective standards to determine qualification should be established and made
known

18. All of the following statements about the *pyramid type* tournament are true EXCEPT: 18.____

    A. It resembles the elimination consolation tournament in structure
    B. It allows for more participation than the ladder tournament
    C. The pyramid tournament can be extended for an indefinite period
    D. Challenges are encouraged in this tournament

19. All of the following statements concerning the stunt *Chinese Pull Up* are true EXCEPT: 19.____

    A. Two opponents sit on the floor facing each other with soles of feet touching
    B. Opponents each grasp a wand or similar stick with either the right or the left hand
    C. A steady pull rather than a varied pull is used
    D. Forcing the opponent to break his hold or pulling him off the floor constitutes a win

20. All of the following are true of the game *Bombardment* EXCEPT: 20.____

    A. Indian clubs or tenpins are set up
    B. A player may throw whenever he receives a ball
    C. If a player steps into the *club base,* the ball is given to an opponent
    D. Players are free to move around in any part of the playing area

21. The term *ace* is associated with all of the following activities EXCEPT   21.____

    A. badminton   B. golf
    C. handball   D. speedball

22. All of the following concerning the playground teacher's plan for the day are recom-   22.____
mended EXCEPT:

A. Alternate plans for indoor activities should be provided in the event of inclement weather
B. Definite time periods for specific activities should be provided and adhered to exactly
C. Children should play an important part in planning
D. Plans should be written out

23. All of the following statements regarding shuffleboard are true EXCEPT: 23.____

    A. Scoring of a disk cannot be determined until all eight disks have been played
    B. Disks that do not pass the farther dead line may remain until all other disks are played
    C. In singles, one round of play shall decide a tie
    D. A disk resting in a scoring area resting on a line does not score

24. Shortly after putting up some elaborate posters announcing tournaments and activities in the playground, you find pencil scribbling over several of them.
Of the following, the BEST way to handle the situation is to   24.____

    A. bring to the direct attention of the group the unfairness of this kind of conduct
    B. remove the posters and inform the class that no prior announcement of activities will be made
    C. erase the scribblings and attempt subsequently to apprehend the culprit
    D. set up a committee of students to ascertain the person or persons responsible

25. In order to secure the GREATEST educational values from a trip planned for a group of twenty-five twelve-year-olds, the playground teacher should   25.____

    A. instruct them carefully in the various rules and regulations to be followed
    B. make the trip himself, before taking the children, for purposes of orienting himself
    C. provide a mimeographed sheet for each child, indicating what is to be seen
    D. encourage parents to assist in conducting the trip

26. All of the following statements about the game of *Long Ball* are true EXCEPT: 26.____

    A. Any touch of the ball with the bat unless caught by a fielder entitles the batter to run to the field base
    B. Only one player may *occupy* the field base at one time
    C. The runner may be *tagged*
    D. No fixed number of players is necessary

27. The term *pyramids* is associated with   27.____

    A. a game of low organization
    B. an activity associated with tumbling
    C. a quiet game
    D. a card game

28. In the activity *Rooster Fight,* each contestant   28.____

    A. grasps his own ankles
    B. assumes any crouched position
    C. keeps his hands on his hips
    D. pushes his opponent with an open hand

29. Of the following, the PRIME responsibility of the first aider is to

    A. apply a splint to a fracture
    B. treat for shock
    C. help the patient to regain consciousness
    D. reduce a dislocation

29._____

30. All of the following are true of the game *End Ball* EXCEPT:

    A. One-third of the members of a team are basemen who stand within the goal area
    B. No player may walk or run with the ball
    C. Players are either basemen or guards
    D. This game emphasizes shooting as opposed to passing

30._____

31. In golf, from an exaggerated open stance, a right-handed golfer's drive will usually

    A. slice
    B. fade to the left
    C. hook
    D. have a long, low trajectory

31._____

32. Of the following scores in table tennis, the one which constitutes a completed game is

    A. 15-13   B. 15-14   C. 21-20   D. 25-23

32._____

33. The same server must serve throughout the game in

    A. badminton   B. team deck tennis
    C. tennis   D. table tennis

33._____

34. All of the following are true of the dual combat contest known as a *Cook Fight* EXCEPT:

    A. Each contestant raises his left foot forward and grasps it with his left hand
    B. The right hand is kept close to the side during the contest
    C. Charging and shouldering are permitted
    D. Points are scored only when a contestant's left foot touches ground

34._____

35. In *Circle Stride Ball,* the player who is *It*

    A. attempts to throw the ball outside the circle in any way possible
    B. tries to throw the ball between the legs of the other players
    C. scores one point if he succeeds in throwing the ball out of the circle
    D. receives only three chances to penetrate the circle with the ball

35._____

36. In teaching a group game, actual playing of the game should begin

    A. only when all the instructional elements of play have been developed by the teacher
    B. after sufficient time has been devoted to developing skills
    C. after a brief description of the game has been given
    D. only when all players are vitally interested

36._____

37. Astigmatism is due PRIMARILY to

    A. a loss of elasticity in the lens
    B. the eyeballs' being too long

37._____

C. an irregularity in the curvature of the eyeball
D. an imbalance of eye muscles

38. Of the following, the area in which student leaders can be MOST helpful to the program is the

    A. supervision of games to insure safety
    B. instruction of slow learners
    C. administering of first aid
    D. selection of subsequent activities

38.____

39. All of the following statements concerning the game *Simon Says* are true EXCEPT:

    A. It is a game in which a leader is required
    B. Originality rather than *following a leader* is stressed
    C. It may be considered either an active or a quiet game
    D. Large numbers of players may participate successfully

39.____

40. The term *nook* is associated with

    A. soccer   B. riflery   C. badminton   D. archery

40.____

41. Of the following pairs of scores in handball, the pair which indicates that the game has been won is

    A. 6-0   B. 11-10   C. 15-13   D. 21-20

41.____

42. All of the following concerning the game *Two Deep* are true EXCEPT:

    A. Both *Two Deep* and *Three Deep* are *tag* games
    B. The action in *Two Deep* is not as rapid as in *Three Deep*
    C. *Two Deep* does not require an even number of players
    D. *Two Deep* utilizes a circle formation

42.____

43. All of the following are true of the game *Overtake* EXCEPT:

    A. Players of one team are arranged in a circle alternately with players of the opposing team
    B. A captain for each team stands in the corner
    C. Passing and catching are required skills
    D. Accuracy of play, not speed, is stressed

43.____

44. Of the following, the LEAST effective use of the last fifteen minutes of the afternoon session in the playground is the

    A. pointing out of individual errors in sports activities made by students throughout the day
    B. discussion and evaluation of the activities of the day
    C. planning of the program for the subsequent day in the playground
    D. providing of time for *cooling off* physiologically

44.____

45. The rules governing table tennis differ from those for lawn tennis in all of the following respects EXCEPT

45.____

A. the number of *faults* allowed in serving
B. volleying
C. the number of points needed to win a game
D. the method of determining the choice of courts

46. *Yards Off, Ring-a-lie-vio, Sardines,* and *Wolf* are classified as games of   46._____

    A. tag   B. hide and seek
    C. tag and hide and seek   D. tag and guessing

47. *All Up Relay* is an activity that involves the use of   47._____

    A. two circles   B. a baseball and bat
    C. two bases   D. a basketball

48. All of the following are authors of excellent books on group games EXCEPT   48._____

    A. Bancroft   B. Mason   C. Mitchell   D. Rice

49. All of the following are correct cues in the teaching of the one-hand side arm pass in basketball EXCEPT: 49._____

    A. Assume a stride stand position, one foot forward, one foot back
    B. Keep an eye on the receiver
    C. Control the speed of the pass
    D. Throw the ball with a wrist snap and avoid the shoulder push

50. All of the following are true of *Batball* EXCEPT: 50._____

    A. It combines elements of baseball and volleyball
    B. The field is divided into a fielding area and a base area
    C. Two goals are used
    D. A runner is out if struck by a ball fairly thrown by a fielder

51. All of the following are true of *Lineball* EXCEPT: 51._____

    A. Two teams line up facing each other on parallel lines drawn forty-five feet apart
    B. Two bats and two baseballs are used
    C. A ball batted over an opponent's head scores a point
    D. Each player gets an opportunity to bat in turn

52. The service in badminton, according to official rules, must be made   52._____

    A. with an underhand motion
    B. with an overhand motion
    C. in a manner mutually agreed upon by opponents prior to the game
    D. in any manner desired by the player

53. All of the following statements are true of the game *Corner Ball* EXCEPT: 53._____

    A. Each corner of the playing area constitutes a goal
    B. Players may cross the center line that divides the court
    C. Players may not walk with the ball
    D. The ball may not be held more than three seconds

54. All of the following statements are true of the game *Crows and Cranes* EXCEPT: 54._____

    A. The commands of the leader are important to the success of the game
    B. Alternate pursuits are characteristic of the game
    C. One goal line is established
    D. It is popular with all age groups

55. In badminton, a winning score in points, common to the men's and women's doubles game, is   55._____

    A. 11   B. 15   C. 20   D. 25

56. Tennis rules differ for men and women with respect to the   56._____

    A. size of the court
    B. number of points in a game
    C. number of games in a set
    D. number of sets in a match

57. In tennis, all of the following cues are correct EXCEPT: 57._____

    A. Try to hit the ball at or after the crest of the bounce
    B. During the execution of a forehand stroke, step into the ball as you start to swing
    C. By slicing the racket face across the ball in the serve you impart a spin on your ball
    D. Force your opponent to the net by using a lob

58. In tennis, a ball which falls on a line is ruled   58._____

    A. a let and should be played over
    B. out of bounds
    C. in play
    D. automatically a point for the opponent

59. Of the following sports, the one BEST suited to co-recreational activity is   59._____

    A. softball   B. kickball
    C. speedball   D. volleyball

60. All of the following are true of volleyball EXCEPT: 60._____

    A. Players do not rotate positions
    B. Six players constitute an official team
    C. If a serve is lost, the ball goes to the opponents
    D. The server may have a retrial at service in the case of a let service

61. All of the following are true of the game of *Touch* EXCEPT: 61._____

    A. A leader indicates a type of object that must be touched
    B. This is always played as an individual rather than team game
    C. This game appeals to many age groups
    D. A large or a small space may be used

62. In tennis, when the score is forty-love, the CORRECT statement with regard to the server is that he   62._____

A. needs one more point to win the game
B. exchanges places with the receiver
C. has won four successive points
D. should be serving from the left-hand court

63. In the four-step delivery, the right-handed bowler should think of all of the following EXCEPT

   63.____

A. taking the first step with his right foot
B. making each succeeding step slightly longer than the previous step
C. releasing the ball with the right foot forward
D. standing the same distance from the foul line at the beginning of each delivery

64. *Indian Chief* is a game that is classified as a _____ game.

   64.____

A. word   B. guessing   C. tag   D. ball

65. All of the following are true of the game *Line Soccer* EXCEPT:

   65.____

A. The ball may be kicked over the heads of the opposing linemen
B. One player from each team at a time moves out to the center area to kick the ball in an effort to score a goal
C. Linesmen may use their hands to stop the ball but are not permitted to throw it
D. A runner may not push, hold, shove, or block the opposing runner

66. *Indian leg wrestling* is performed in a _____ position.

   66.____

A. standing   B. crouching   C. supine   D. prone

67. The total number of contests required to complete an elimination tournament for seven teams with a consolation series for the first round losers is

   67.____

A. eight   B. ten   C. twelve   D. fourteen

68. All of the following statements are true of the pyramid type of tournament EXCEPT:

   68.____

A. The pyramid offers a wider choice of opponent than the ladder type does
B. A player may challenge any player higher in the pyramid
C. A pyramidal type of tournament requires a time limit
D. The pyramid may be successfully used in individual or team competition

69. Of the following, the statement concerning byes in an elimination tournament which is CORRECT is:
Byes

   69.____

A. may be provided in either the first or the second round
B. may be provided in any round except the last
C. are given to the best players
D. occur only in the first round

70. All of the following are true of the game *Chinese Wall* EXCEPT:

   70.____

A. Ten feet separate the two imaginary walls
B. This is a game suitable for younger as well as older children

C. A space approximately 90 ft. by 30 is required to play it effectively
D. The game is played by organizing two teams equal in number of players

71. In an 18 hole golf match, a *5* and *3* victory will have been won upon completing the _____ hole.   71.____

A. 13th   B. 14th   C. 15th   D. 16th

72. The number of games to schedule, in order to complete a round robin tournament for eight teams, is   72.____

A. 16   B. 20   C. 24   D. 28

73. All of the following are true of the stunt *Badger Pull* EXCEPT: 73.____

A. Two towels tied together at either end are used as a collar
B. Opponents kneel facing each other equally distant from a line drawn between them
C. The object of the stunt is to pull the opponent over the midline
D. If the collar slips off, it is replaced without penalty

74. When a strike is rolled in the 10th frame of a bowling game, the bowler   74.____

A. continues to bowl two more frames
B. is allowed to roll his second ball to complete the frame
C. completes the game by rolling 2 additional balls
D. adds 20 points to his game score

75. A bowler who looks at the pins when bowling is called a _____ bowler.   75.____

A. spot   B. line
C. pin   D. straight-ball

KEY (CORRECT ANSWERS)

1. B	16. B	31. A	46. B	61. B
2. D	17. A	32. D	47. A	62. A
3. D	18. A	33. C	48. D	63. C
4. C	19. B	34. A	49. D	64. B
5. A	20. D	35. B	50. C	65. A
6. B	21. D	36. C	51. C	66. C
7. A	22. B	37. C	52. A	67. A
8. A	23. B	38. B	53. B	68. B
9. A	24. C	39. B	54. C	69. D
10. B	25. B	40. D	55. B	70. D
11. A	26. B	41. D	56. D	71. C
12. B	27. B	42. B	57. D	72. D
13. C	28. A	43. D	58. C	73. D
14. C	29. B	44. A	59. D	74. C
15. A	30. D	45. D	60. A	75. C

EXAMINATION SECTION

TEST 1

DIRECTIONS: Each question consists of a statement. You are to indicate whether the statement is TRUE (T) or FALSE (F). *PRINT THE LETTER OF THE CORRECT ANSWER IN THE SPACE AT THE RIGHT.*

Questions 1-7.

DIRECTIONS: Questions 1 through 7 are to be answered SOLEY on the basis of the information contained in the following paragraph.

RESPONSIBILITY OF PARENTS

In a recent survey, ninety percent of the people interviewed felt that parents should be held responsible for the delinquency of their children. Forty-eight out of fifty states have laws holding parents criminally responsible for contributing to the delinquency of their children. It is generally acceptged that parents are a major influence in the early moral development of their children. Yet, in spite of all this evidence, practical experience seems to prove that "punish the parents" laws are wrong. Legally, there is some question about the constitutionality of such laws. How far can one person be held responsible for the actions of another? Further, although there are many such laws, the fact remains that they are rarely used, and where they are used they fail in most cases to accomplish the end for which they were intended.

1. Nine out of ten of those interviewed held that parents should be reponsible for the delinquency of their children.   1.____

2. Forty-eight percent of the states have laws holding parents responsible for contributing to the delinquency of their children.   2.____

3. Most people feel that parents have little influence on the early moral development of their children.   3.____

4. Experience seems to indicate that laws holding parents responsible for children's delinquency are wrong.   4.____

5. There is no doubt that laws holding parents responsible for delinquency of their children are within the Constitution.   5.____

6. Laws holding parents responsible for delinquent children are not often enforced.   6.____

7. "Punish the parent" laws *usually* achieve their purpose.   7.____

Questions 8-13.

DIRECTIONS: Questions 8 through 13 are to be answered SOLELY on the basis of the information contained in the following paragraphs.

CONTROL OF RABIES

The history of rabies in many countries proveds the need for strong preventive measures. England is a good example. Rabies ran rampant in the British Isles during the American Revolution. In the 19th Century, the country began to enforce stric measures: licensing of all dogs, muzzling all dogs and quanrantining all incoming animals for 6 months' observation. An additional measure was the capturing and killing of all unlicensed "strays."

As a result, rabies was completely eradicated, and similar measures have achieved the same results in Ireland, Denmark, Norway, Sweden, Australia, and Hawaii.

8.   Rabies was prevalent in England around the year 1776.   8._____

9.   By enforcement of strict measures in the 1800's, rabies was eliminated in   9._____
     England.

10. The only measures enforced in England for the control of rabies were the   10._____
     licensing and muzzling of all dogs.

11. Unlicensed dogs without owners were put to death when found.   11._____

12. A total of six countries, including England, obtained good results in   12._____
     combating rabies.

13. Rabies has been eliminated in three Scandinavian countries.   13._____

Questions 14-25.

DIRECTION: Questions 14 through 25 are to be answered SOLELY on the basis of the information contained in the following paragraphs.

RESCUE BREATHING

"Mouth-to-mouth," or "rescue breathing," is the easiest, most efficient, and quickest method of getting oxygen into a suffocating victim of drowning, heart attack, electricl shock, poisoning or other cause of interruption of breathing. It is superior to other types of artificial respiration because the victim does not have to be moved and the rescuer can continue for hours without exhaustion. No special equipment is needed.

Begin rescue breathing immediately. The victim's head should be lower than his body. Tilt his head back as far as possible so his jaw juts out. Keep the air passage to his lungs straight at all times. Open your mouth as wide as possible and seal your lips over the adult victim's mouth or his nose and the child victim's mouth and nose. Blow in air until his chest rises. Remove your mouth and listen to him breathe out. Then blow again and fill his lungs.

For the first minute, blow thirty times into a child, then twenty times a minute. With an adult, blow twenty times for the first minute, then ten to twelve times a minute. Do not stop breathing for the victim, however long it takes, until he begins breathing for himself – or is dead.

14. The FASTEST wasy to get oxygen into the lungs of a suffocating person is by mouth-to-mouth breathing.

14.____

15. The "rescue breathing" method of artificial respiration should be used ONLY in cases of drowning.

15.____

16. Rescue breathing is NOT the only kind of artificial respiration.

16.____

17. The person who applies mouth-to-mouth breathing will NOT tire easily.

17.____

18. Special equipment used in rescue breathing should be kept handy at all times.

18.____

19. Rescue breathing should be commenced at the earliest possible moment.

19.____

20. The suffocating victim should be placed so that his body is NOT higher than his head.

20.____

21. In "rescue breathing," the head of the victim should be bent forward so oxygen will be more easily forced in the lungs.

21.____

22. In mouth-to-mouth breathing, air may be blown into the victim's nose.

22.____

23. When "rescue breathing" is applied to children, air should be blown into the lungs thirty times djuring the first minute.

23.____

24. It is NEVER necessary to continue rescue breathing for longer than about five minutes.

24.____

25. Mouth-to-mouth breathing is ALWAYS successful in reviving the victim.

25.____

Questions 26-45.

DIRECTIONS: Questions 26 through 45 relate to word meaning.

26. "His ideas about the best method of doing the work were flexible." In this sentence, the word "flexible" means NEARLY THE SAME as "unchangeable".

26.____

27. "Many difficulties were encountered." In this sentence, the word "encountered" means NEARLY THE SAME as "met".

27.____

28. "The different parts of the refuse must be segregated." In this sentence, the word "segregated" means NEARLY THE SAME as "combined".

28.____

29. "The child was obviously hurt." In this sentence, the word "obviously" means NEARLY THE SAME as "accidentally".   29._____

30. "Some kind of criteria for judging service necessity must be established." In this sentence, the word "criteria" means NEARLY THE SAME as "standards".   30._____

31. "A small segment of the membership favored the amendment." In this sentence, the word "segment" means NEARLY THE SAME as "part".   31._____

32. "The effectiveness of an organization depends upon the quality and integrity of its rank and file." In this sentence, the word "integrity" means NEARLY THE SAME as "quantity".   32._____

33. "He adhered to his opinion." In this sentence, the word "adhered" means NEARLY THE SAME as "stuck to".   33._____

34. "The suspects were interrogated at the police station." In this sentence, the word "interrogated" means NEARLY THE SAME as "identified".   34._____

35. "Flanking the fireplace are shelves holding books." In this sentence, the word "flanking" means NEARLY THE SAME as "above".   35._____

36. "He refused to comment on the current Berlin crisis." In this sentence, the word "current" means NEARLY THE SAME as "shocking".   36._____

37. "Nothing has been done to remedy the situation." In this sentence, the word "remedy" means NEARLY THE SAME as "correct".   37._____

38. "The reports had been ignored." In this sentence, the word "ignored" means NEARLY THE SAME as "prepared".   38._____

39. "A firm was hired to construct the building." In this sentence, the word "construct" means NEARLY THE SAME as "build".   39._____

40. "The commissioner spoke about the operations of his department. In this sentence, the word "operations" means NEARLY THE SAME as "problems."   40._____

41. "The metal was corroded." In this sentence, the word "corroded" means NEARLY THE SAME as "polished".   41._____

42. "The price of this merchandise fluctuates from day to day." In this sentence, the word "fluctuates" means the OPPOSITE of "remains steady".   42._____

43. "The patient was in acute pain." In this sentence, the word "acute" means the OPPOSITE of "slight".   43._____

44. "The essential data appear in the report." In this sentence, the word "data" means the OPPOSITE of "facts". 44.____

45. "The open lounge is spacious." In this sentence, the word "spacious" means the OPPOSITE of "well-lighted". 45.____

46. A good first aid measure for a person who has fainted is to place his head lower than the rest of his body. 46.____

47. Many accidents are caused by carelessness of employees while at work. 47.____

48. If, at work, you are unable to lift a very heavy object, you should rest a couple of minutes and try again. 48.____

49. A victim of a bad fall who has suffered some broken bones should be moved to a comfortable spot *immediately*. 49.____

50. The safest and quickest way to remove a burned out light bulb from a ceiling fixture is to stand on a chair on top of a desk or table. 50.____

51. The legal age for voting in New York State was reduced to 18 years. 51.____

52. The purpose of a primary election is to select party candidates for the general election. 52.____

53. If three men working at the same rate of speed finish a job in 4½ hours, then two of them could do the job in 6¾ hours. 53.____

54. If a typist shares four boxes of envelopes with four other typists, each will have one box of envelopes. 54.____

55. An article bought for $100 must be sold for $125 in order to make a profit of 20% of the selling price. 55.____

56. ½ of ⅛ is ¼. 56.____

57. Ten square feet of carpet will cover the floor of a room 10 feet by 10 feet. 57.____

Questions 58-65.

DIRECTION: Questions 58 through 65 are to be answered SOLELY on the basis of the information contained in the following table.

SUMMONS RECORD

District	No. of Summonses Issued		No. of Summonses Dismissed	
	2014	2015	2014	2015
Oakdale	3,250	3,147	650	631
Marlboro	2,410	2,320	670	718
Eastchester	3,502	3,710	800	825
Kensington	10,423	10,218	2,317	2,343
Glendridge	5,100	5,250	1,200	1,213
Seaside	4,864	4,739	1,469	1,375
Darwin	3,479	3,661	815	826
Ulster	4,100	3,789	1,025	1,000
Totals	37,128	?	8,946	?

58. In most of the districts, the number of summonses dismissesd was GREATER in 2015 than in 2014.   58._____

59. In most of the districts, the number of summonses issued was SMALLER in 2014 than in 2015.   59._____

60. The district which had the SMALLEST number of summonses issued in 2014 also had the SMALLEST number of summonses dismissed in 2014.   60._____

61. The two districts which issued the LARGEST number of summonses in 2015 also dismissed the LARGEST number of summonses in 2015.   61._____

62. The district that was second in the number of summonses issued both years was also second in the number of summonses dismissed both years.   62._____

63. The total number of summonses dismissed in 2015 is 15 less than the total number dismissed in 2014.   63._____

64. In 2015 there was a greater difference between the two districts with the smallest and largest number of summonses dismissesd than in 2014.   64._____

65. The total number of summonses issued in 2014 is 294 GREATER than the total number of summonses issued in 2015.   65._____

KEY (CORRECT ANSWERS)

1.	T	16.	T	31.	T	46.	T	61.	F
2.	F	17.	T	32.	F	47.	T	62.	F
3.	F	18.	F	33.	T	48.	F	63.	T
4.	T	19.	T	34.	F	49.	F	64.	T
5.	F	20.	F	35.	F	50.	F	65.	T
6.	T	21.	F	36.	F	51.	F		
7.	F	22.	T	37.	T	52.	T		
8.	T	23.	T	38.	F	53.	T		
9.	T	24.	F	39.	T	54.	F		
10.	F	25.	F	40.	F	55.	T		
11.	T	26.	F	41.	F	56.	F		
12.	F	27.	T	42.	T	57.	F		
13.	T	28.	F	43.	T	58.	T		
14.	T	29.	F	44.	F	59.	F		
15.	F	30.	T	45.	F	60.	F		

———

TEST 2

DIRECTIONS: Each question or incomplete statement is followed by several suggested answers or completions. Select the one that BEST answers the question or completes the statement. *PRINT THE LETTER OF THE CORRECT ANSWER IN THE SPACE AT THE RIGHT.*

Questions 1-20.

DIRECTIONS: Each of Questions 1 through 20 consists of a word in capital letters followed by four suggested meanings of the word. Select the word or phrase which means MOST NEARLY the same as the word in capital letters.

1. ABRUPT   1.____
    A. smooth   B. safe   C. sudden   D. slow

2. ALLEVIATE   2.____
    A. relieve   B. join   C. agree with   D. raise

3. ALLOT   3.____
    A. permit   B. assign   C. exclude   D. accept

4. ALTER   4.____
    A. divide   B. argue   C. opposite   D. change

5. APPARENT   5.____
    A. unimportant   B. obvious   C. connected   D. loose

6. BRITTLE   6.____
    A. easily broken   B. narrow
    C. made of metal   D. shiny

7. CAPSIZE   7.____
    A. protest   B. press down   C. overturn   D. fill

8. CONSPICUOUS   8.____
    A. colorful   B. point out   C. cooperate   D. noticeable

9. CONSTRICT   9.____
    A. collect   B. compress   C. convince   D. circulate

10. DELETE   10.____
    A. follow   B. refuse   C. hesitate   D. erase

11. FLUCTUATE   11.____
    A. fill gradually   B. change continually
    C. take apart   D. shake loose

12. IMPLY   12.____
    A. excuse   B. fold over   C. examine   D. suggest

13. MAINTAIN   13.____
    A. slow down   B. draw back   C. keep up   D. damage

14. OBSCURE   14.____
    A. empty   B. at an angle   C. receive   D. not clean

15. SCRUTINIZE   15.____
    A. ask politely   B. without mistakes
    C. look at carefully   D. do on purpose

16. SEVER   16.____
    A. separate   B. shift   C. serious   D. strict

17. SPHERICAL   17.____
    A. doubtful   B. round   C. at the edge   D. balanced

18. TAUT   18.____
    A. tight   B. thick   C. tall   D. timely

19. TERMINATE   19.____
    A. stop   B. investigate   C. speed up   D. prefer

20. VARIABLE   20.____
    A. questionable   B. hard   C. changeable   D. responsible

Questions 21-25.

DIRECTIONS: Each of Questions 21 through 25 consists of four sentences. One of the sentences in each group contains an error in grammar, sentence structure or English usage. For each question, select the sentence which is INCORRECT.

21. A.   The driver of the north-bound car, who was responsible for the accident,   21.____
          escaped without injury.
    B.   The Duncan parking meter was the better of the two meters used in the test.
    C.   After a long day of driving, he was real tired.
    D.   The car appeared suddenly over the top of the hill.

22. A.   The man stopped his work because the sun was very hot.   22.____
    B.   The car sped down the road it suddenly swerved toward the ditch along the side of the road.
    C.   On today's modern highways there are many cars; some are new and others are fit only for the junkyard.
    D.   Traffic congestion is a current problem which is hard to solve.

23. A.   Neither the driver nor the pedestrian are to blame for the accident.   23.____
     B.   In his report he included all the pertinent data.
     C.   A new set of rules and regulations has been adopted.
     D.   He asserted that there was no basis for the motorist's complaint of unequal
          treatment.

24. A.   Standing or stopping at an intersection is a violation of the law.   24.____
     B.   Reckless driving, especially at sunset, is a major cause of accidents.
     C.   Before starting a car, you should adjust the rear view mirror and fasten
          your seat belt.
     D.   Pulling up at the gas station, the gas tank was filled up before they began
          their trip.

25. A.   Because the accident report was incomplete, a question arose as to who   25.____
          was at fault.
     B.   They told both he and I that the suggestion was accepted.
     C.   He was allowed to choose whomever he wanted for the job.
     D.   The final decision was reached after everyone told his side of the incident.

Questions 26-30.

DIRECTIONS: Each of Questions 26 through 30 consists of a group of four words. Examine
              each group carefully, then in the space at the right, print one of the following
              letters:
                   A – if only ONE word in the group is spelled correctly.
                   B – if TWO words in the group are spelled correctly.
                   C – if THREE words in the group are spelled correctly.
                   D – if ALL FOUR words in the group are spelled correctly.

26. Wendsday, particular, similar, hunderd   26.____

27. realize, judgment, opportunities, consistent   27.____

28. equel, principle, assistense, commitee   28.____

29. simultaneous, privilege, advise, ocassionaly   29.____

30. necissery, official, Febuary, distence   30.____

Questions 31-37.

DIRECTIONS: Questions 31 through 37 are to be answered on the basis of the information
              given in the following passage.

The parking meter was designed 30 years ago primarily as a mechanism to assist in
reducing parking overtime at the curb, to increase parking turnover, and to facilitate
enforcement of parking regulations. That the meter has accomplished these basic functions is
attested to by its use in an increasing number of cities.

A recent survey of cities in the United States indicates that overtime parking was reduced 75% or more in 47% of the cities surveyed, and to a lesser degree in 43% of the cities surveyed, making a total of 90% of the cities surveyed where the parking meter was found to be effective in reducing overtime parking at the curb.

A side effect of the reduction in overtime parking is the increase in parking turnover. Approximately 89% of the places surveyed found meters useful in this respect. Meters also encourage even spacing of cars at the curb. Unmetered curb parking is often so irregular that it wastes space or makes parking and departure difficult.

The effectiveness of parking meters, in the final analysis, rests upon the enforcement of the regulations by squads of enforcement agents who will diligently patrol the metered area. The task of checking parking time is made easier with meters, since violations can be checked from a moving vehicle or by visual sightings of an agent on foot patrol, and the laborious process of chalking tires is greatly reduced. It is reported that, after meters have been installed, it takes on the average only 25% of the time formerly required to patrol the same area.

The fact that a parker activates a mechanism that immediately begins to count time, that will indicate exactly when the parking time has expired, and that will advertise such a fact by showing a red flag, tends to make a parker more conscious of his parking responsibilities than the hit and miss system of possible detection by a patrolman.

31. According to the above passage, when the parking meter was introduced, one of its major purposes was NOT to   31.____
   - A. cut down overtime curb parking
   - B. make curb parking available to more parkers
   - C. bring in revenue from parking fees
   - D. make it easier to enforce parking regulations

32. In the cities surveyed, the installation of parking meters   32.____
   - A. was *effective* to some degree in all the cities surveyed
   - B. was *ineffective* in only 1 out of every 10 cities surveyed
   - C. *reduced* overtime parking at least 75% in most cities surveyed
   - D. *slightly reduced* overtime parking in 43% of the cities surveyed

33. When overtime parking is reduced by the installation of parking meters, an accompanying result is   33.____
   - A. an increase in the amount of parking space
   - B. the use of the available parking spaces by more cars
   - C. the faster the movement of traffic
   - D. a decrease in the number of squads required to enforce traffic regulations

34. According to the above passage, on streets which have parking meters, as compared with streets with are un-metered,   34.____
   - A. there is less waste of parking space
   - B. parking is more difficult
   - C. parking time limits are irregular
   - D. drivers waste more time looking for an empty parking space

35. According to the above passage, the use of parking meters will NOT be   35.____
    effective unless
    A. parking areas are patrolled in automobiles
    B. it is combined with chalking of tires
    C. the public cooperates
    D. there is strict enforcement of parking regulations

36. According to the above passage, ONE reason why there is greater   36.____
    compliance with parking regulations when parking time is regulated by meter
    rather than by a foot patrolman chalking tires is that
    A. overtime parking becomes glaringly evident to everyone
    B. the parker is himself responsible for operating the timing mechanism
    C. there is no personal relationship between parker and enforcing officer
    D. the timing of elapsed parking time is accurate

37. In the last paragraph of the above passage, the words "a parker activates   37.____
    a mechanism" refers to the fact that a motorist
    A. starts the timing device of the meter working
    B. parks his car
    C. checks whether the meter is working
    D. starts the engine of his car

Questions 38-40.

DIRECTIONS: Questions 38 through 40 are to be answered on the basis of the information
              given in the following passage.

    When markings upon the curb or the pavement of a street designate parking space, no
person shall stand or park a vehicle in such designated parking space so that any part of such
vehicle occupies more than one such space or protrudes beyond the markings designating such
a space, except that a vehicle which is of a size too large to be parked within a single
designated parking space shall be parked with the front bumper at the front of the space with
the rear of the vehicle extending as little as possible into the adjoining space to the rear, or vice-
versa.

38. The regulations quoted above applies to parking at ANY   38.____
    A. curb or pavement   B. metered spaces
    C. street where parking is permitted   D. spaces with marked boundaries

39. The regulations quoted above PROHIBITS the occupying of more than one   39.____
    indicated parking space by
    A. any vehicle
    B. large vehicles
    C. small vehicles
    D. vehicles in spaces partially occupied

40. In the regulations quoted above, the term "vice-versa" refers to a vehicle of   40.____
   a size too large parked with
   A. front bumper flush with front of parking space it occupies
   B. front of vehicle extending into front of parking space
   C. rear bumper flush with rear of parking space it occupies
   D. rear of vehicle protruding into adjoining parking space

---

KEY (CORRECT ANSWERS)

1.	C	11.	B	21.	C	31.	C
2.	A	12.	D	22.	B	32.	B
3.	B	13.	C	23.	A	33.	B
4.	D	14.	D	24.	D	34.	A
5.	B	15.	C	25.	B	35.	D
6.	A	16.	A	26.	B	36.	A
7.	C	17.	B	27.	D	37.	A
8.	D	18.	A	28.	A	38.	D
9.	B	19.	A	29.	C	39.	C
10.	D	20.	C	30.	A	40.	C

PREPARING WRITTEN MATERIAL

PARAGRAPH REARRANGEMENT
COMMENTARY

The sentences which follow are in scrambled order. You are to rearrange them in proper order and indicate the letter choice containing the correct answer at the space at the right.

Each group of sentences in this section is actually a paragraph presented in scrambled order. Each sentence in the group has a place in that paragraph; no sentence is to be left out. You are to read each group of sentences and decide upon the best order in which to put the sentences so as to form as well-organized paragraph.

The questions in this section measure the ability to solve a problem when all the facts relevant to its solution are not given.

More specifically, certain positions of responsibility and authority require the employee to discover connections between events sometimes, apparently, unrelated. In order to do this, the employee will find it necessary to correctly infer that unspecified events have probably occurred or are likely to occur. This ability becomes especially important when action must be taken on incomplete information.

Accordingly, these questions require competitors to choose among several suggested alternatives, each of which presents a different sequential arrangement of the events. Competitors must choose the MOST logical of the suggested sequences.

In order to do so, they may be required to draw on general knowledge to infer missing concepts or events that are essential to sequencing the given events. Competitors should be careful to infer only what is essential to the sequence. The plausibility of the wrong alternatives will always require the inclusion of unlikely events or of additional chains of events which are NOT essential to sequencing the given events.

It's very important to remember that you are looking for the best of the four possible choices, and that the best choice of all may not even be one of the answers you're given to choose from.

There is no one right way to solve these problems. Many people have found it helpful to first write out the order of the sentences, as they would have arranged them, on their scrap paper before looking at the possible answers. If their optimum answer is there, this can save them some time. If it isn't, this method can still give insight into solving the problem. Others find it most helpful to just go through each of the possible choices, contrasting each as they go along. You should use whatever method feels comfortable, and works, for you.

While most of these types of questions are not that difficult, we've added a higher percentage of the difficult type, just to give you more practice. Usually there are only one or two questions on this section that contain such subtle distinctions that you're unable to answer confidently, and you then may find yourself stuck deciding between two possible choices, neither of which you're sure about.

EXAMINATION SECTION
TEST 1

DIRECTIONS: The sentences that follow are in scrambled order. You are to rearrange them in proper order and indicate the letter choice containing the correct answer. *PRINT THE LETTER OF THE CORRECT ANSWER IN THE SPACE AT THE RIGHT.*

1. Below are four statements labeled W., X., Y., and Z.   1.____
   W.   He was a strict and fanatic drillmaster.
   X.   The word is always used in a derogatory sense and generally shows resentment and anger on the part of the user.
   Y.   It is from the name of this Frenchman that we derive our English word, martinet.
   Z.   Jean Martinet was the Inspector-General of Infantry during the reign of King Louis XIV.
   The *PROPER* order in which these sentences should be placed in a paragraph is:

   A.   X, Z, W, Y   B.   X, Z, Y, W   C.   Z, W, Y, X   D.   Z, Y, W, X

2. In the following paragraph, the sentences which are numbered, have been jumbled.   2.____
   1.   Since then it has undergone changes.
   2.   It was incorporated in 1955 under the laws of the State of New York.
   3.   Its primary purpose, a cleaner city, has, however, remained the same.
   4.   The Citizens Committee works in cooperation with the Mayor's Inter-departmental Committee for a Clean City.
   The order in which these sentences should be arranged to form a well-organized paragraph is:

   A.   2, 4, 1, 3   B.   3, 4, 1, 2   C.   4, 2, 1, 3   D.   4, 3, 2, 1

Questions 3-5.

DIRECTIONS: The sentences listed below are part of a meaningful paragraph but they are not given in their proper order. You are to decide what would be the *best order* in which to put the sentences so as to form a well-organized paragraph. Each sentence has a place in the paragraph; there are no extra sentences. You are then to answer questions 3 to 5 inclusive on the basis of your rearrangements of these scrambled sentences into a properly organized paragraph.

In 1887 some insurance companies organized an Inspection Department to advise their clients on all phases of fire prevention and protection. Probably this has been due to the smaller annual fire losses in Great Britain than in the United States. It tests various fire prevention devices and appliances and determines manufacturing hazards and their safeguards. Fire research began earlier in the United States and is more advanced than in Great Britain. Later they established a laboratory specializing in electrical, mechanical, hydraulic, and chemical fields.

3. When the five sentences are arranged in proper order, the paragraph starts with the sentence which begins

    A. "In 1887 ..."   B. "Probably this ..."   C. "It tests ..."
    D. "Fire research ..."   E. "Later they ..."

    3.____

4. In the last sentence listed above, "they" refers to

    A. insurance companies
    B. the United States and Great Britain
    C. the Inspection Department
    D. clients
    E. technicians

    4.____

5. When the above paragraph is properly arranged, it ends with the words

    A. "... and protection."   B. "... the United States."
    C. "... their safeguards."   D. "... in Great Britain."
    E. "... chemical fields."

    5.____

KEY (CORRECT ANSWERS)

    1. C
    2. C
    3. D
    4. A
    5. C

TEST 2

DIRECTIONS: In each of the questions numbered 1 through 5, several sentences are given. For each question, choose as your answer the group of numbers that represents the *most logical* order of these sentences if they were arranged in paragraph form. *PRINT THE LETTER OF THE CORRECT ANSWER IN THE SPACE AT THE RIGHT.*

1. 1. It is established when one shows that the landlord has prevented the tenant's enjoyment of his interest in the property leased.
    2. Constructive eviction is the result of a breach of the covenant of quiet enjoyment implied in all leases.
    3. In some parts of the United States, it is not complete until the tenant vacates within a reasonable time.
    4. Generally, the acts must be of such serious and permanent character as to deny the tenant the enjoyment of his possessing rights.
    5. In this event, upon abandonment of the premises, the tenant's liability for that ceases.

    The CORRECT answer is:

    A. 2, 1, 4, 3, 5   B. 5, 2, 3, 1, 4   C. 4, 3, 1, 2, 5
    D. 1, 3, 5, 4, 2

    1.____

2. 1. The powerlessness before private and public authorities that is the typical experience of the slum tenant is reminiscent of the situation of blue-collar workers all through the nineteenth century.
    2. Similarly, in recent years, this chapter of history has been reopened by anti-poverty groups which have attempted to organize slum tenants to enable them to bargain collectively with their landlords about the conditions of their tenancies.
    3. It is familiar history that many of the workers remedied their condition by joining together and presenting their demands collectively.
    4. Like the workers, tenants are forced by the conditions of modern life into substantial dependence on these who possess great political arid economic power.
    5. What's more, the very fact of dependence coupled with an absence of education and self-confidence makes them hesitant and unable to stand up for what they need from those in power.

    The CORRECT answer is:

    A. 5, 4, 1, 2, 3   B. 2, 3, 1, 5, 4   C. 3, 1, 5, 4, 2
    D. 1, 4, 5, 3, 2

    2.____

3. 1. A railroad, for example, when not acting as a common carrier may contract away responsibility for its own negligence.
    2. As to a landlord, however, no decision has been found relating to the legal effect of a clause shifting the statutory duty of repair to the tenant.
    3. The courts have not passed on the validity of clauses relieving the landlord of this duty and liability.
    4. They have, however, upheld the validity of exculpatory clauses in other types of contracts.
    5. Housing regulations impose a duty upon the landlord to maintain leased premises in safe condition.

    3.____

6. As another example, a bailee may limit his liability except for gross negligence, willful acts, or fraud.

The CORRECT answer is:

A. 2, 1, 6, 4, 3, 5   B. 1, 3, 4, 5, 6, 2   C. 3, 5, 1, 4, 2, 6
D. 5, 3, 4, 1, 6, 2

4.

1. Since there are only samples in the building, retail or consumer sales are generally eschewed by mart occupants, and in some instances, rigid controls are maintained to limit entrance to the mart only to those persons engaged in retailing.
2. Since World War I, in many larger cities, there has developed a new type of property, called the mart building.
3. It can, therefore, be used by wholesalers and jobbers for the display of sample merchandise.
4. This type of building is most frequently a multi-storied, finished interior property which is a cross between a retail arcade and a loft building.
5. This limitation enables the mart occupants to ship the orders from another location after the retailer or dealer makes his selection from the samples.

The CORRECT answer is:

A. 2, 4, 3, 1, 5   B. 4, 3, 5, 1, 2   C. 1, 3, 2, 4, 5
D. 1, 4, 2, 3, 5

5.

1. In general, staff-line friction reduces the distinctive contribution of staff personnel.
2. The conflicts, however, introduce an uncontrolled element into the managerial system.
3. On the other hand, the natural resistance of the line to staff innovations probably usefully restrains over-eager efforts to apply untested procedures on a large scale.
4. Under such conditions, it is difficult to know when valuable ideas are being sacrificed.
5. The relatively weak position of staff, requiring accommodation to the line, tends to restrict their ability to engage in free, experimental innovation.

The CORRECT answer is:

A. 4, 2, 3, 1, 3   B. 1, 5, 3, 2, 4   C. 5, 3, 1, 2, 4
D. 2, 1, 4, 5, 3

KEY (CORRECT ANSWERS)

1. A
2. D
3. D
4. A
5. B

TEST 3

DIRECTIONS: Questions 1 through 4 consist of six sentences which can be arranged in a logical sequence. For each question, select the choice which places the numbered sentences in the *most logical* sequence. *PRINT THE LETTER OF THE CORRECT ANSWER IN THE SPACE AT THE RIGHT.*

1.   1. The burden of proof as to each issue is determined before trial and remains upon the same party throughout the trial.   1.____
   2. The jury is at liberty to believe one witness' testimony as against a number of contradictory witnesses.
   3. In a civil case, the party bearing the burden of proof is required to prove his contention by a fair preponderance of the evidence.
   4. However, it must be noted that a fair preponderance of evidence does not necessarily mean a greater number of witnesses.
   5. The burden of proof is the burden which rests upon one of the parties to an action to persuade the trier of the facts, generally the jury, that a proposition he asserts is true.
   6. If the evidence is equally balanced, or if it leaves the jury in such doubt as to be unable to decide the controversy either way, judgment must be given against the party upon whom the burden of proof rests.

   The CORRECT answer is:

   A. 3, 2, 5, 4, 1, 6   B. 1, 2, 6, 5, 3, 4   C. 3, 4, 5, 1, 2, 6
   D. 5, 1, 3, 6, 4, 2

2.   1. If a parent is without assets and is unemployed, he cannot be convicted of the crime of non-support of a child.   2.____
   2. The term "sufficient ability" has been held to mean sufficient financial ability.
   3. It does not matter if his unemployment is by choice or unavoidable circumstances.
   4. If he fails to take any steps at all, he may be liable to prosecution for endangering the welfare of a child.
   5. Under the penal law, a parent is responsible for the support of his minor child only if the parent is "of sufficient ability."
   6. An indigent parent may meet his obligation by borrowing money or by seeking aid under the provisions of the Social Welfare Law.

   The CORRECT answer is:

   A. 6, 1, 5, 3, 2, 4   B. 1, 3, 5, 2, 4, 6   C. 5, 2, 1, 3, 6, 4
   D. 1, 6, 4, 5, 2, 3

3.   1.   Consider, for example, the case of a rabble rouser who urges a group of twenty   3.____
           people to go out and break the windows of a nearby factory.
     2.   Therefore, the law fills the indicated gap with the crime of inciting to riot.
     3.   A person is considered guilty of inciting to riot when he urges ten or more per-
           sons to engage in tumultuous and violent conduct of a kind likely to create public
           alarm.
     4.   However, if he has not obtained the cooperation of at least four people, he can-
           not be charged with unlawful assembly.
     5.   The charge of inciting to riot was added to the law to cover types of conduct
           which cannot be classified as either the crime of "riot" or the crime of "unlawful
           assembly."
     6.   If he acquires the acquiescence of at least four of them, he is guilty of unlawful
           assembly even if the project does not materialize.
   The CORRECT answer is:

   A. 3, 5, 1, 6, 4, 2   B. 5, 1, 4, 6, 2, 3   C. 3, 4, 1, 5, 2, 6
   D. 5, 1, 4, 6, 3, 2

4.   1.   If, however, the rebuttal evidence presents an issue of credibility, it is for the jury to   4.____
           determine whether the presumption has, in fact, been destroyed.
     2.   Once sufficient evidence to the contrary is introduced, the presumption disap-
           pears from the trial.
     3.   The effect of a presumption is to place the burden upon the adversary to come
           forward with evidence to rebut the presumption.
     4.   When a presumption is overcome and ceases to exist in the case, the fact or
           facts which gave rise to the presumption still remain.
     5.   Whether a presumption has been overcome is ordinarily a question for the court.
     6.   Such information may furnish a basis for a logical inference.
   The CORRECT answer is:

   A. 4, 6, 2, 5, 1, 3   B. 3, 2, 5, 1, 4, 6   C. 5, 3, 6, 4, 2, 1
   D. 5, 4, 1, 2, 6, 3

KEY (CORRECT ANSWERS)

      1. D
      2. C
      3. A
      4. B

BASIC FUNDAMENTALS OF SPORTS

CONTENTS

BASIC FUNDAMENTALS OF SPORTS

PRINCIPLES OF ATHLETICS

Athletics in the Physical Training Program

❖ Athletics deserve a prominent place in the physical training program because they contribute to the increased efficiency of the student. Because of the competitive nature of athletics and their natural appeal, the students take part in them with enthusiasm. Athletic teams formed at the intramural and higher levels are a strong unifying influence and provide one of the best means of developing esprit de corps.

❖ The athletic sports selected must be vigorous to insure good conditioning value.

❖ All the components of physical fitness cannot be developed with athletics alone. These sports are beneficial primarily in sustaining interest in the program and maintaining a level of physical fitness. Therefore, athletics are to be considered as a supplement and not a substitute for the less interesting conditioning drills.

BASKETBALL

INTRODUCTION

Basketball has enjoyed increased popularity and growth within the past few years, unequaled by any other American sport. It should be comparatively easy for an instructor to create interest in basketball among student personnel, both for conditioning and recreational purposes. Few sports have the potentialities that basketball has for developing coordination, endurance, skill, teamwork, and the will to win. It is an excellent activity for the sustaining stage. One of the objectives of a physical training program is 100 percent participation. A well-organized basketball program makes it possible to more nearly accomplish this objective than any other athletic activity.

BASIC SKILLS

Men prefer to play rather than practice so, whenever possible, a part of each instruction period should be devoted to a scrimmage game. To prevent the loss of program interest, the instructor should vary the practice routine, add new plays, organize tournaments, and devise other ways to maintain enthusiasm. He should use textbooks written by professional basketball coaches to plan and teach offensive and defensive plays.

A. **Fundamentals**
   I. Shooting baskets.
      a. One-hand set shots. Shoot from a balanced position. Keep both feet on the floor. Follow through
      b. Two-hand set shots. Shoot from a balanced position and apply equal pressure on the ball with each hand. Keep both feet on the floor. Follow through.
      c. Lay-ups. Jump high, reach high before releasing the ball. Spin the ball, using the backboard when possible.
      d. Shooting while on move. This is usually a one-handed shot. Shoot off opposite foot from the hand that releases the ball.
      e. Jump shot. Jump high, release ball with one hand at apex of height. Most common shot today.
      f. Free throws. These are one-hand and two-hand underhand throws and two-hand push shots. Put a slight back spin on the ball.

2. Ball-handling.
   a. Two-hand chest pass. Step in the direction of the pass. Use a wrist action to release the ball with a back spin.
   b. One-hand and two-hand bounce pass. Step in the direction of the pass. Bounce the ball a reasonable distance in front of the receiver, putting a back spin on the ball with a wrist action.
   c. One-hand baseball pass. Step in the direction of the pass; throw as you would throw a baseball. This is used mostly for long passes.
   d. Two-hand overhead pass. Hold the ball above the head with the arms extended. Throw with a wrist action. This pass is used mainly to get the ball to the pivot man who is close to the basket.

3. Dribbling.
   a. Changing hand with ball. Only one hand may touch the ball at one time while dribbling. The hands may be alternated.
   b. Change of pace. Changing speed and direction while dribbling.
   c. Dribbling exercise with eyes not directly on ball. Change direction; change hands; keep the head up with the eyes directed toward possible passing or shooting situations.

4. Footwork.
   a. Pivoting. Give the pivotman or center special practice in pivoting. One foot remains stationary while the opposite foot is mobile.
   b. Individual defense. Stress footwork and the position of the hands and body.
   c. Check position of feet when shooting various types of shots. Points to check: the position of balance; correct foot forward when in shooting position; the distance between each foot.

B. Small Group or Team Practice.
1. Man-to-man defense.
   1) Switching. Each defensive man is responsible for defending against a designated man, until a screen or block forces the defensive man to change defensive responsibility.
   2) Nonswitching. Each defensive man is responsible for a designated man with the defensive man going through or behind screens and blocks.
2. Man-to-man offense. Various types of offensive formations have been especially designed to combat man-to-man defense. Use textbooks written by professional coaches for technical knowledge.
3. Zone defense. There are numerous variations of this type defense aimed at defending a restricted area in front of the basket. The defensive target is the ball, not the man.
4. Zone offense. The zone offense forces the defense to adjust position, as a unit, rapidly and often. Zone offense is most effective when employing rapid movement of the ball within the defense area.
5. Defense against fast break. Stress rebound work on the offensive backboard. Stress court balance by offensive team.
6. Fast break offense. Move down court into scoring or offensive territory quickly.

PRACTICE DRILLS

Some practice routines are -

a. Keep-Away. Divide unit into two groups. Designate each individual's defensive responsibility by name or number. Use half of a basketball court as the playing area. The team in possession of the ball passes it among the team members until the defense gets possession of it. Basketball rules apply. Continue with each team taking turns as it gets possession of the ball.

b. Shooting Exercise. Divide unit into small groups. Each group has a ball. Designate the various positions on the floor where the shooting practice is to be done. Use a pre-arranged scoring method. Play numerous games, giving each group an opportunity to shoot from all positions on the floor.

c. Dribbling Exercise. Divide unit into two or three groups. Each group has a ball. Conduct a dribbling relay. Place obstacles for dribblers to avoid and designate the path each team will follow.

d. Defense Exercises. Use the two free throw circles and the restraining circle at center court. Place five men around the outside of each circle. One man is in the center of each ring. It is the job of the man in the center to intercept or deflect the path of the ball which is passed from man to man by the men outside of the circle. No pass may be made to an adjacent man in the circle. When the man inside the circle succeeds in intercepting, deflecting, or touching the ball, the passer takes his place.

FACILITIES AND EQUIPMENT

a. Facilities. In some sections of the country, outdoor facilities may be used, and they are easily constructed. The minimum dimensions of a court for competition are approximately 74 feet by 42 feet; maximum dimensions are 94 feet by 50 feet.

b. Equipment. A basketball is the only required equipment. For highly organized competition, however, uniforms, special shoes, and other equipment may be required.

RULES

So-called college rules or, more correctly, The National Collegiate Athletic Association rules, are used in conducting basketball in the physical training program. Each year a new paper-bound guide booklet is published and sold by the NCAA.

———

CROSS-COUNTRY AND DISTANCE RUNNING

INTRODUCTION

a. Long-distance running gives some benefits that cannot be obtained in the same degree from any other sport. It builds powerful leg muscles, increases the lung capacity, and develops endurance. For these reasons, cross-country and distance running should be included in the physical training program. These sports require only a few miles of open space that is available at school. They do require time, however, and many physical training supervisors do not find it feasible to use them as individual full-time sports. Short cross-country runs and middle-distance runs can be used to supplement other activities, particularly the team sports or the sports that develop precision or agility rather than endurance. Short cross-country runs can be scheduled once a week, gradually increasing the distance as the physical condition of the men improves; or distance running can be combined with other activities such as the conditioning exercises.

b. Cross-country and the distance runs do not enjoy equal popularity with other sports, for obvious reasons. They require great endurance, and endurance requires months of rigid training. There is a common belief that long-distance running is too strenuous, often resulting in permanent injury to the heart. While distance running may be harmful to the man who overdoes the sport, when he is not in proper physical condition, the conditioned, supervised distance runner is in no greater danger of strain than the man engaged in any other athletic activity.

LONG-DISTANCE RUNS

Any run over a mile is classed as a long-distance run. The instructor may vary the distance of the run during the season, or he may standardize it at whatever length will best suit his men or the facilities available to him. Two miles is the most popular distance. Often, the two-mile run is included as an event in track and field meets, but more frequently it is treated as a separate sport. The two-mile run may be run on any type of flat outdoor course, on a regular cinder track, or on a grass or dirt course. Because the ground is often frozen too hard for long-distance running during cold weather, the two-mile run is not recommended as a winter activity except in mild climates. The sport is too strenuous for very hot weather. The run cannot be held indoors. Constant pounding of the feet on the hard surface causes shin splints and injuries to the ankle joints.

CROSS-COUNTRY RUNS

Cross-country is a distance run held on a course laid out along roads, across fields, over hills, through woods, on any irregular ground. A flat cinder or dirt track is not a suitable surface for cross-country running. Opinions vary as to the proper length of a cross-country course. Some runs are as long as six miles. Five miles used to be accepted as standard, but recently there has been a tendency to shorten the run to four or even three miles. Only if time is available for a full-season cross-country program should the physical training instructor try to train men for a five-mile course. If time is limited, or if cross-country running is being used to supplement other activities, the three-mile course is long enough for most men.

PLACE IN THE PROGRAM

Cross-country and distance running should be used only after the men reach the sustaining stage of conditioning. They should then be scheduled occasionally to provide variety in the program. Cross-country running has the advantage of allowing mass participation. Interest can be stimulated by putting the runs on a competitive basis.

BASIC SKILLS

a. Cross-Country Running Form. Running form in cross-country races varies with the terrain and the contour of the course. On the flat, use the same form as used in a two-mile run. The body lean should be between 5 and 10 percent. A lean of more than 10 percent places too much weight and strain on the legs. A lean of less than 5 percent is retarding. In running uphill, lean forward at a greater angle and cut the length of the stride. To gain an added lift, swing the arms high and bring the knees up high on each stride. Do not slow down after reaching the crest of the hill, but resume the flat course stride as soon as the ground levels off. The runner's stride will naturally lengthen in going downhill, but he should not stretch his stride or increase his pace too much. There is less control and less balance when running downhill;

therefore, there is greater danger of turning an ankle and of falling. Keep the arms low, swinging freely, and use them as a brake and as a balance. Coming onto the flat from a downhill run, do not slow down but float or coast into a flat course pace. More energy will be used in attempting to brake the speed of descent than in maintaining the faster pace and slowing down gradually. Run on the toes or the balls of the feet, rather than on the heels. Landing on the heels throughout a five-mile course would jolt the entire body injuriously. Runners who have a tendency to strike the heel on the ground should wear a cotton or sponge rubber pad in the heels of their shoes, unless their footgear has rubber heels.

    b. Racing Tactics for Cross-Country.

        1) Teams can be pitted against each other in cross-country races. Certain members of the team may need encouragement along the way. If the team runs well-bunched for most of the course, the stronger runners can lead and encourage the weaker men. The pace should be scaled to the pace of the average runner on the team. Within a mile of the finish, however, the group should break and each man run out the race for himself.

        2) If the coach prefers his team to run on an individual basis, there are several techniques for outwitting opponents. A good runner may not take the lead but stay behind an opponent and conserve his energy for the final sprint. The opponent may tire himself out trying to maintain the lead and become so discouraged when passed by a strong sprint near the finish that he will not fight to reach the tape first. If leading an opponent, a runner may discourage him by constantly increasing the lead when he is out of sight. Opportunities for doing this frequently occur at corners of the course obscured by trees or bushes. If the leading runner sprints a short distance after rounding the corner, he may increase his lead 10 or 15 yards. After this has happened two or three times, an easily discouraged opponent may cease to be a serious contender for the race.

PRACTICE METHODS

    a. Conditioning is more essential to distance and cross-country running than to any other sport. Championship distance running depends on stamina, and stamina can be developed only through constant training. A man of only average ability can become an outstanding distance runner by steady and careful training. Hiking is the best method for getting into condition before the season opens. Long walks build up the leg muscles. During the first month of the season, training should be gradual, starting with short distances and increasing day by day. At first, the legs will become stiff, but the stiffness gradually disappears if running is practiced for a while every day. To prevent strain, it is essential to limber up thoroughly each day before running.

    b. In the mass training of a large group, leaders should be stationed at the head and the rear of the column, and they should make every effort to keep the men together. After determining the abilities of the men in cross-country running, it is advisable to divide the unit into three groups. The poorest conditioned group is started first, the best conditioned group, last. The starting time of the groups should be staggered so that all of them come in about the same time. In preliminary training, the running is similar to ordinary road work in that it begins with rather slow jogging, alternating with walking. The speed and distance of the run is gradually increased. As the condition of the men improves, occasional sprints may be introduced. At first, the distance run is from one-half to one mile. It is gradually increased to two or three miles. On completing the run, the men should be required to continue walking for three or four minutes before stopping, to permit a gradual cooling off and return to normal physiological functioning.

FACILITIES AND EQUIPMENT

a. A course three or five miles long should be measured and marked by one of the three methods specified below:

    1) Directional arrows fastened to the top of a tall post and placed at every point where the course turns. Such signs should also be placed at every other point where there may be doubt as to the direction of travel.

    2) A lime line placed on the ground over the entire course.

    3) Flags. They should be clearly visible to the runners.

        a) A red flag indicates a left turn.

        b) A white flag indicates a right turn.

        c) A blue flag indicates the course is straight ahead.

b. There should be at least one stopwatch (preferably three) for timing the runners.

RULES

    a) Team Members. A cross-country team shall consist of seven men, unless otherwise agreed. In dual meets, a maximum of twelve men may be entered, but a maximum of seven shall enter into the scoring.

    b) Scoring. First place shall score 1 point, second place 2, third place 3, and so on. All men who finish the course shall be ranked and tallied in this manner. The team score shall then be determined by totaling the points scored by the first five men of each team to finish. The team scoring the least number of points shall be the winner.

    Note: Although the sixth and seventh runners of a team to finish do not score points toward their team's total, it should be noted that their places, if better than those of any of the first five of an opposing team, serve to increase the team score of the opponents.

    c) Cancellation of Points. If less than five (or the number determined prior to the race) finish, the places of all members of that team shall be disregarded.

    d) Tie Event. In case the total points scored by two or more teams result in a tie, the event shall be called a tie.

———

SOCCER

INTRODUCTION

a.   Soccer is one of the best athletic activities for developing endurance, agility, leg strength, and a great degree of skill in using the legs. The game is the most popular sport in Europe and is the national game of many of the Central and South American countries. In recent years, it has become popular in United States schools and colleges.

b.   A soccer ball is the only equipment needed for the game, and the men can learn to play it easily. The men do not need much skill to participate, but the amount they can develop is unlimited.

PLACE IN THE PROGRAM

Soccer should be introduced into the physical training program during the latter part of the slow improvement stage and used as a competitive activity in the sustaining stage. It is primarily a spring or fall sport. Any level field is suitable for competition. The boundaries for the soccer field are similar to the dimensions for a football field. Goal posts are essential to the game, but they are easily constructed and are usually of a temporary nature, so that they may be removed when not in use.

BASIC SKILLS

a.   Passing. Passing with the feet is the basic means of moving the ball. Short passes are easier to control and can be done more accurately than long ones. Emphasis should be continually placed on skill in passing.

b.   Dribbling. The ball is dribbled by a series of kicks with the inside or outside of the foot. Do not kick with the toe. Keep the head over the ball when kicking and propel it only a short distance at a time. Keep it close to the feet. When the ball gets very far from the feet while dribbling, an opposing player can easily take it away.

c.   Instep Kicking. The instep kick, which is the basic soccer kick, is made from the knee joint instead of from the hip as in football. The toe does not come in contact with the ball. It is pointed downward and the instep (the shoe laces) is applied to the ball with a vigorous snap from the knee. For a stationary ball, the non-kicking foot is alongside the ball at the time of the kick. For a ball rolling toward the kicker, his non-kicking foot stops short of the ball; for a ball rolling away from the kicker, his non-kicking foot stops beyond the ball. The kicker must keep his eye on the ball until it has left his foot.

d.   Inside-of-the-Foot Kicking. The ball is kicked with the inside of the foot and the leg is swung from the hip. The toe is turned outward and the sole of the boot is parallel with the ground as the foot strikes the ball. The ball should be well under the body at the time of contact. This kick is used for short passes and for dribbling.

e.   Foot Trapping. The foot trap is the method of stopping the ball by trapping it between the ground and the foot. Place the sole of the foot on top of the ball at the instant it touches the ground, but do not stamp on it. Keep the foot relaxed. This is an effective way to stop a high-flying ball.

f.   Shin Trapping. The shin trap is a method of stopping the ball with the shins. Stand just forward of the spot where the ball should strike the ground and allow it to strike the shins in flight or on the bounce. Use either one or both legs from the knee down, but do not allow the ball to strike the toe.

g.   Body Trapping. The body trap is another method of gaining control of a ball in flight. Intercept the ball with any part of the upper body except the arms and hands. Keep the body relaxed and inclined toward the ball. To keep the ball from bouncing, move backward from it as it strikes the body. This will drop the ball at the feet in position for dribbling or passing.

h.   Heading. Heading is the technique for changing the direction of the flight of a ball by butting it with the head. Tense the neck muscles and jump up to meet the ball. Butt the ball with the forehead at about the hairline to reverse its direction; use the side of the head to deflect it to the side. Always watch the ball, even during contact

OFFENSIVE AND DEFENSIVE POSITIONS

The forwards usually play on the offensive half of the field and remain in a W formation. The fullbacks usually play on the defensive half of the field. The halfbacks are the backbone of the team; they move forward on the offense and back on defense. The goal keeper almost always remains within a few feet of the goal.

DRILLS TO DEVELOP BASIC SKILLS

Several drills are recommended to develop skill in kicking, passing, and shooting. The circle formation may be used for training in any of the basic skills. The ball may be headed or trapped as it is moved around or across the circle.

ABRIDGED RULES

a. A soccer team is composed of eleven players.

b. The player propels the ball by kicking it with the feet or any part of the legs, by butting it with his head, and by hitting it with any portion of his body except his arms or hands.

c. The goalkeeper is the only man allowed to use his hands on the ball, but he may only handle the ball in the goalkeeper's area. The term hands includes the whole arm from the point of the shoulder down.

d. A goal is made by causing the ball to cross completely the section of the goal line lying between the uprights and under the cross bar.

e. Each goal scores one point for the team scoring the goal.

f. The penalty for a foul committed anywhere on the playing field (except by the defensive team in its penalty area) is a free kick awarded to the team that committed the foul.

g. All opponents must be at least 10 yards from the ball when a free kick is taken.

h. The penalty for a foul committed by the defensive team in its penalty area is a penalty kick.

i. A penalty kick is a free kick at the goal from the spot 12 yards directly in front of the goal. The only players allowed within the penalty area at the time of the kick are the kicker and the defending goalkeeper.

j. An official game consists of four quarters.

k. Teams change goals at the end of every quarter.

l. In the event of a tie, an extra quarter is played.

m. After a ball has crossed a side line and has been declared out of play, it is put back into play by a free kick from the side line by a member of the team opposing the team that caused the ball to be out of bounds. The kick is taken from the point at which the ball crosses the side line as it goes out of bounds.

n. When the offensive team causes the ball to go behind the opposing team's goal line, excluding the portion between the goal posts, the opposing team is awarded a goal kick - a free kick taken within the goal area that must come out of the penalty area to be in play.

o. When the defensive team causes the ball to go behind its own goal line, excluding the portion between the goal posts, the opposing team is awarded a corner kick - a free kick taken by a member of the offensive team at the quarter circle at the corner flag-post nearest to where the ball went behind the goal line. The flag-post must not be removed.

p. The game is started and, after a goal has been scored, is resumed by placing the ball in the center of the mid-field line. Players must be on their side of the line until the ball is kicked. The ball must be kicked forward and must move at least two feet to be legal. The first kicker may not touch the ball twice in succession at the kick-off. The opposing team must be ten yards from the ball until it moves.

SOFTBALL

INTRODUCTION

a. Softball is a game that is known in every corner of the country and has become a familiar sight in every sandlot in America. During and since World War II, it has become one of the principal physical training activities.

b. Softball is patterned after baseball, but has different advantages because it requires less equipment and is easily adapted to every age group. It requires a smaller play area; the ball is larger and softer; and the bats are lighter, making them easier to handle. Because of its popularity, a majority of our young people have a general understanding of softball and softball rules, but only a comparative few possess the skill and knowledge to obtain the maximum benefit and satisfaction from the game.

PLACE IN THE PROGRAM

a. Softball is a sustaining type of activity. It does not require continuous exertion on the part of each player; however, it is an enjoyable and occasionally strenuous game that should be included in the physical training program.

b. When a group already knows something about pitching, fielding, and batting, the instructor should give only a brief review of these fundamental skills, but place more emphasis on the rules and offensive and defensive strategy. Most of the time devoted to softball should be used for organized competition.

ORGANIZATION OF INSTRUCTION

When instruction is given on the basic skills and techniques, the students should first be shown the correct method of executing each skill. The class should then be divided into groups to practice. Ample time should be provided to familiarize each individual with the technique of playing each position as well as the basic skills necessary to play every position. When this instruction is completed, the class should be divided into teams for organized competition.

BASIC SKILLS

a. Batting. Select a bat that balances easily - hands grasp the handle at a point where the butt is neither too heavy nor too light. For a right-handed batter, the left foot points at about a 45° angle toward the pitcher, and the right foot points toward homeplate. The feet are about 8 inches apart. The head and eyes face the pitcher, and the bat is over the right shoulder, hands away from the body. The batting position is slightly to the rear of the center of the plate. In swinging, keep the eyes on the ball, twisting at the waist. As a result of the twist, the arms will swing automatically. The power of the swing is developed with a snap of the wrists and the extension of the arms in the follow-through.

b. Bunting. The stance for bunting is the same as for batting. When the ball leaves the pitcher's hand, immediately bring the bat from over the shoulder, moving the right hand slightly up the handle, until the bat is directly over the plate. Rotate the body so that it faces the pitcher. The feet are comfortably apart. Meet the ball squarely, absorbing the shock with the arms. Hold the edge of the bat perpendicular to the direction in which the ball is to be bunted.

c. Base Running. Upon hitting the ball, the runner must start quickly without watching where the ball goes. He should get to the first base as fast as possible and be ready to continue running at the coach's direction. Speed is the most important factor, but running the shortest distance between bases is also essential.

d. Sliding. Use the hook slide going into the base, with the body relaxed, extending either foot in a sweeping motion, touching the toe to the bag.

e. Catching. Assume the knee bend position, with the upper arms parallel to the ground, forearms vertical, and palms down. As the ball strikes the mitt, grasp it with the bare hand. On high pitches, cup the fingers of the bare hand to prevent injury. On low pitches, extend the palms toward the pitcher with the thumbs down. Always avoid pointing the fingers toward the pitcher. The catcher must not sacrifice accuracy for speed in throwing to bases and must learn through experience when he can throw a player out at base.

f. Pitching. Pitching, to a large degree, determines a team's defensive strength, and pitching can only be developed through practice. To hold the ball, grasp it loosely with the fingers, the index, middle, and third fingers on one side and the thumb and fourth finger on the other side. The most effective manner of pitching is the windmill pitch. To start the wind-up, face the homeplate with both feet on the rubber. The ball is held in front with both hands. Raise the left foot to the rear as the right arm swings backward. The body pivots to the right, the left hand is extended and balances the motion, and the head and eyes remain on the catcher's glove. When the right arm reaches the nine o'clock position, step forward with the left foot directly toward homeplate, swing the arm forward, and twist the body to the left. With a snap of the wrist on the underhand swing, release the ball and follow through. Control is very important and must be gained through practice.

g. Infield Playing. An infielder must anticipate at all times what he should do in case he has to play the ball. On batted ground balls, he should play the ball to his front. Field each ground ball with the feet apart, hands well out in front. When the ball strikes the glove, secure it with the bare hand. The hands and arms should relax, and the arms should be drawn backward toward the right hip preparatory to the throw.

h. Outfield Playing. An outfielder should be alert and fast and able to judge the ball so he can get in the best position to catch it. It takes practice to become a successful fielder. To catch a fly ball, he extends the arms forward, forming a cup with the hands. He keeps his eyes on the ball until he has firm possession of it. He catches ground balls in the same way as the infielder (see g. above).

DRILLS

a. Pitching and Catching. Divide the class into two lines fifty feet apart; one side will pitch, the other will catch. Make corrections on form for both pitching and catching. Emphasize form and control. Change over.

b. Infield Play. Divide the class into seven-man groups. Place each group in a separate area, simulating (if necessary) the softball diamond. Designate a first, second, and third baseman, and a shortstop. Choose one man to hit balls and one to catch at homeplate. The player who hits balls first calls a play such as first base, double play, throw it home, etc. He then hits a ground ball to one of the infielders who, in turn, carries out the prescribed play. Demand enthusiasm and hustle. Change over occasionally and allow each man to play each position.

c. Outfield Play. Place seven men in the outfield, but do not designate definite positions. Have a player hit both fly and ground balls to the field. Use one player to catch balls at homeplate. After each ball has been played, have it relayed back to the hitter. Change positions so that each player has an opportunity to play in the outfield.

d. Base Running. Divide the class into fifteen-man groups. Time each runner in a complete circuit of bases. Stimulate competition. Critique each runner.

e. Hitting and Bunting. Divide the class into regular nine-man teams. Place one team in the field to shag balls. The players on the other team take turns at bat, hitting ten balls each. On the last pitch, they lay down a bunt and run to first base, trying to beat the throw. Change over.

OFFENSIVE AND DEFENSIVE STRATEGY

a. Offensive. Hit only good balls (balls in the strike zone). Runners should run out fly balls at top speed, in case the ball is dropped or an error is committed. There is a better possibility of stealing a base than of the next batter hitting safely. Do not hesitate in stealing. Do not attempt to steal third base when two men are out, because a runner should be able to score from second base on a hit or on an error. It is best to attempt to steal second base with two outs. With no outs and runners on first and second base, a bunt combined with a double steal is good strategy. A runner can usually score from third base on a fly ball or on an error.

b. Defensive. A player should always back up another player receiving a throw at a base, or a player attempting to make a play on a fly or ground ball. The player who is nearest the ball should call for it and make the catch or play. Each player should be aware of the situation and know exactly what to do if he receives the ball. Receive bunts, flys, and ground balls with both hands. Have firm possession of the ball before attempting a throw. On force plays, do not stand on the base. It is better to make certain of one out, rather than risk an error in trying for a double play. When a shorter throw can put a runner out at base, it is best to attempt the shorter throw. With runners on first and second base, it is better to force out at third than to try a double play from second to first base. An outfielder should throw the ball directly to the spot where the play is likely to be made, unless it is a long fly and a relay appears to be quicker.

SPEEDBALL

INTRODUCTION AND GENERAL DESCRIPTION

Speedball is a game that offers vigorous and varied action with plenty of scoring opportunities. It is easy to learn and provides spontaneous fun. Little equipment is needed - a ball is all that is absolutely necessary. Speedball combines the kicking, trapping, and intercepting elements of soccer; the passing game of basketball; and the punting, drop-kicking, and scoring pass of football. Two teams of eleven men each play the game under official rules, but any number of players may successfully constitute a team. An inflated leather ball, usually a soccer ball, is used. The playing field is a football field with a football goal post at each end. The game starts with a soccer-type kickoff. The kicking team tries to retain possession of the ball and advance it toward the opposite goal by passing or kicking it. Running with the ball is not allowed, so there is no tackling or interference. When the ball touches the ground, it cannot be picked up with the hands or caught on the bounce, but must be played as in soccer until it is raised into the air directly from a kick; then the hands are again eligible for use. When the ball goes out of bounds over the side lines, it is given to a player of the team opposite that forcing the ball out, and is put into play with a basketball throw-in; when it goes over the end line without a score, it is given to a player of the opposing team who may either pass or kick it onto the field. When two opposing players are contesting the possession of a held ball, the official tosses the ball up between them as in basketball. Points are scored by kicking the ball under the crossbar of the goal posts, drop-kicking the ball over the crossbar, completing a forward pass into the end zone for a touchdown, or by kicking the ball under the crossbar of the goal posts on a penalty kick.

PLACE IN THE PROGRAM

Speedball, like soccer, should be introduced into the physical training program during the latter part of the toughening stage and used as a competitive activity in the sustaining stage. It may be played any time the weather permits, but it is primarily a spring or fall activity.

BASIC SKILLS

   a. Soccer Techniques.
       i. Kicking.
       ii. Passing.
       iii. Heading.
       iv. Trapping.
   b. Football Techniques.
       i. Punting.
       ii. Drop-kicking.
       iii. Forward passing.
   c. Basketball Techniques.
       i. Passing.
       ii. Receiving.
       iii. Pivoting.
   d. Kickups and Lifts. The kickup is a play in which a player lifts the ball into the air with his feet so that he may legally play the ball with his hands. The kickup is generally used to make the transition from ground play to aerial play. The technique of making the play depends upon whether the ball is rolling or stationary. To kick up a ball rolling or bouncing toward the player, the foot is held on the ground with the toe drawn down until the ball rolls onto the foot, then the foot is raised, projecting the ball upward. If the ball is stationary, the player rolls it backward with one foot, then places the foot where the ball will roll onto it. He can then lift the ball with that foot. If a ball is rolling away from the player, he should stop it with a foot and play it as a stationary ball. There is also a method of raising the ball by standing over it with a foot on either side. He presses his feet against the ball and jumps into the air, propelling the ball into his hands.

OFFENSIVE POSITIONS AND STRATEGY

The positions of the players in speedball are much the same as in soccer. However, some of the positions are designated by different names. There are eleven players on each team. The forward line is composed of five players: the right end, right forward, center, left forward, and left end. The second line consists of right halfback, fullback, and left halfback. In the next line is the right guard and left guard. The player who defends the_ goal is the goal guard. The strategy employed in speedball during offensive play is very similar to that of soccer.

DEFENSIVE PLAY

There are two types of defensive formations in speedball: man-for-man and position defense. Man-for-man defense is recommended for beginning players.

ABRIDGED RULES

    a.   The Field. 360 feet long and 160 feet wide (a regulation football field).

    b.   Players. Eleven on a team. The goal guard has no special privileges.

    c.   Time. Ten-minute quarters, two minutes between. Ten minutes between halves. Five minutes for extra overtime periods. (Begin first overtime by a jump ball (see g(3) below) at center, same goals; change goals in the event of a second overtime period.)

    d.   Winner of Toss. The winner of the toss has the choice of kicking, receiving, or defending a specific goal.

    e.   Starting Second and Fourth Quarters. The ball is given to the team that had possession at the end of the previous quarter, out of bounds, as in basketball.

    f.   Half. The team that received at the start of the first half kicks off at the beginning of the second half.

    g.   The Game. The game is started with a kickoff from the middle line (50-yard line), both teams being required to remain back of their respective restraining lines until the ball is kicked. The ball must travel forward.

        1.   The most characteristic feature of the playing rules of speedball is the differentiation between a fly ball (or aerial ball) and a ground ball. A player is not permitted to touch a ground ball with his hands and must play it as in soccer. A fly ball is one that has risen into the air directly from the foot of a player (example: punt, drop-kick, place-kick, or kickup). Such a ball may be caught with the hands provided the catch is made before the ball strikes the ground again. A kickup is a ball that is so kicked by a player that he can catch it himself. A bounce from the ground may not be touched with the hand because it has touched the ground since being kicked. This rule prohibits the ordinary basketball dribble, but one overhead dribble (throwing the ball into the air and advancing to catch it before it hits the ground) is permitted.

        2.   If a team causes the ball to go out of bounds over the side lines, a free throw-in (any style) is given to the opposing team. When the ball goes over the end line without scoring, it is given to the opponents who may pass or kick from out of bounds at that point.

        3.   In case two players are contesting the possession of a held ball, even in the end zone, a tie ball is declared and the ball is tossed up between them.

        4.   The kick-off is made from any place on or behind the 50-yard line. Team A (the kicking team) must be behind the ball when it is kicked. Team B must stay back of its restraining line (ten yards' distance) until the ball is kicked (penalty - a violation). The ball must go forward before A may play it (penalty - violation). Kick off out of bounds to opponents at that spot. A kick-off touched by B and going out of bounds, no impetus added, still belongs to B. A kick-off, in possession and control of B and then fumbled out of bounds, belongs to A at that spot. A field goal from kick-off (under crossbar, etc.) scores 3 points.

h. Scoring Methods.
  1. Field goal (3 points). A soccer-type kick, in which a ground ball is kicked under the crossbar and between the goal posts from the field of play or end zone. (A punt going straight through is not a field goal for it is not a ground ball. The ball must hit the ground first.) A drop-kick from the field of play that goes under a crossbar does not count as a field goal. A drop-kick from the end zone that goes under the crossbar counts as a field goal; if it goes over the crossbar, it is ruled as a touch back.
  2. Drop-kick (2 points). A scoring drop-kick must be made from the field of play and go over the crossbar and between the uprights. The ball must hit the ground before it is kicked (usually with the instep).
  3. End goal (1 point). This is a ground ball which receives its impetus (kicked or legally propelled by the body) from any player, offensive or defensive, in the end zone and passes over the end line but not between the goal posts.
  4. Penalty kick (1 point). This is a ball kicked from the penalty mark that goes between the goal posts and under the crossbar. The penalty mark is placed directly in front of the goal at the center of the goal line.
  5. Touchdown (1 point). A touchdown is a forward pass from the field of play completed in the end zone. The player must be entirely in the end zone. If he is on the goal line or has one foot in the field of play and the other in the end zone, the ball is declared out of bounds. If a forward pass is missed, the ball continues in play but must be returned to the field of play before another forward pass or drop-kick may be made.
i. Substitutions. Substitutions may be made any time when the ball is not in play. If a player is withdrawn, he may not return during that same period.
j. Time Out. Three legal time-outs of two minutes each are permitted each team during the game.
k. Fouls.
  1. Personal (four disqualify). Kicking, tripping, charging, pushing, holding, blocking, or unnecessary roughness of any kind, such as running into an opponent from behind. Kicking at a fly ball and thereby kicking an opponent.
  2. Technical. Illegal substitution, more than three time-outs in a game, unsportsmanlike conduct, unnecessarily delaying the game.
  3. Violation. Traveling with the ball, touching a ground ball with the hands or arms, double overhead dribble, violating tie ball, and kicking or kneeing a fly ball before catching it.
  4. Penalties. (The offended player shall attempt the kick.)

	Penalty	Location
Personal	In field of play	1 kick with no follow-up
Technical	In field of play	1 kick with no follow-up
Violation	In field of play	Out of bound to opponent
Personal	In end zone	2 kick with no follow-up on last kick
Technical	In end zone	1 kick with no follow-up
Violation	In end zone	1 kick with no follow-up

l. Summary of Fouls.
  1. Fouls in the field of play allow no follow-up while fouls in the end zone always allow follow-up.
  2. On penalty kicks, with no follow-up, only the kicker and goalie are involved.
  3. On penalty kicks, with a follow-up, the kicking side is behind the ball and the defending side behind the end line or in the field of play. No one is allowed in the end zone or between the goal posts except the goal guard. The kicker cannot play the ball again until after another player plays it, and he must make an actual attempt at goal.

TOUCH FOOTBALL

INTRODUCTION

Touch football has become a major active game on the lower levels of competition. Considering its similarity to football and yet its comparative simplicity, it is easy to understand the popularity of the game. The modification of regulation football rules for touch football eliminates the necessity for much special equipment, training, and professional leadership. Touch football encourages participation, reduces the number of injuries, and simplifies the teaching of fundamental rules, techniques, and skills.

PLACE IN THE PROGRAM

Touch football is an excellent conditioning activity, and it should be included in both the physical training and intramural programs. It may be used in the latter part of the toughening stage and during the sustaining stage of physical conditioning. It should be played in the fall when the interest in football is at its peak. Any level field can be used. Goal posts are desirable but not absolutely necessary.

ORGANIZATION OF INSTRUCTION

Most men know something about football, but not all have had an opportunity to play. Several short periods should be devoted to the instruction of all men in the basic fundamentals. A desirable method is to give five to ten minutes of instruction at the beginning of each football period and follow it by actual play.

BASIC SKILLS

a. Offensive Stance. Touch football emphasizes speed; therefore, a high offensive stance should be used to facilitate a fast getaway. The feet should be about shoulder width apart and parallel, knees bent, thighs just above the horizontal and back nearly parallel with the ground. The head and eyes are up, and the right hand is extended straight downward, the fingers curled under, the thumb toward the rear. The left arm rests on the left thigh. There are many variations of this basic stance that may be used. The general principles are: Keep the feet spread for balance, the body under control, and the head up with the eyes on an opponent or the ball.

b. Defensive Stance. This type stance may be similar to the offensive stance or somewhat higher to allow for better visibility and free use of the hands to ward off blockers. The same principles of balance, body control, and vision used in the offensive stance are applicable to the defensive stance.

c. Blocking. Touch football rules do not permit the blocker to have both feet off the ground at the same time (flying block); therefore, the blocker should maintain a wide base for shoulder, upright, or cross-body blocks. For the shoulder block, the hands should be close to the chest, the elbows raised sideward, the feet under the body and widely spread, the head up, and the buttocks low. Upon contact, the feet should be moved rapidly in short, choppy steps to force the body forward, thus keeping the shoulder in contact with the opponent. The upright block is useful in the open field and is executed by the player while standing nearly erect. The feet are widely spread, knees slightly bent, the trunk inclined slightly forward, and the head erect. The arms are raised, and the hands are placed on the chest, forearms forward to contact the opponent. Due to the nature of the block, the opponent is contacted above the waist. In performing the cross-body block, the blocker uses the hip to contact the opponent, usually in the area of the thighs. The execution of this type of block requires the blocker to throw his head, shoulders, and arms past the target area, thus bringing his hip into contact with his opponent. Then, assisted by movement of the hands and feet which are in contact with the ground, he forces the opponent backward or down. The shoulder, upright, or cross-body blocks may be used in the line or in the open field.

d. Ball Carrying. The first point to stress in ball carrying is the grip of the ball. The ball is placed in the arm with its long axis parallel to the forearm. It is held firmly and close to the body. The hand grips the lower point of the ball with the fingers spread to form a firm grip. It is difficult to teach the fine points of ball carrying in a few hours of instruction. Stress the principles. Teach runners to carry the ball in the arm away from the opponent. The runner should be cautioned to follow his interference and to keep his head up so he can avoid his opponents.

e.   Forward Passing. Forward passing is one of the principal means of advancing the ball in touch football. Teach the method of gripping or holding the ball with the fingers spread on the laces and toward the end of the ball, cocking the arm with the hand holding the ball close to the head and the wrist rotated so that the rear point of the ball is pointing toward the head. The ball is delivered with a baseball catcher's peg motion, by extending the arm and imparting a spiral to the ball. To make a successful forward pass, it is usually best for the passer to have the feet spread comfortably and in contact with the ground, the free hand extended to aid the balance. He throws the ball to a spot where the receiver can catch it without breaking his stride. Do not allow beginners to attempt jump passes, as the successful throwing of this type of pass requires the skill of an experienced forward passer.

f.   Pass Receiving. To catch a forward pass requires the receiver to keep his eyes on the ball, to run to the spot where he can reach the ball, to catch it without breaking stride, and to take it out of the air by relaxing the hands as the ball strikes. In receiving a pass over the shoulder, the little fingers are facing, with the thumbs outward and all fingers spread. In catching a pass while facing the passer, the receiver should catch a high pass with the thumbs facing and the little fingers out; and a low pass with the little fingers facing and the thumbs pointing outward.

DRILLS TO DEVELOP FUNDAMENTALS

It is recommended that the time available for instruction in the fundamentals be used in teaching the following skills: stance, shoulder block, cross-body block, forward passing, and pass receiving.

a.   Stance Drill. Use the extended rectangular formation. Demonstrate the stance and tell the men they will execute the drill by the numbers. At the count of one, place the feet in position. At the count of two, bend the knees and trunk. At the count of three, lean forward and place one hand on the ground. After checking for errors and making corrections, command "UP" and execute the drill again. Have the men do this several times before progressing to the next drill.

b.   Blocking Drills. All the blocks may be practiced by forming the class into two lines facing one another and having the men pair off. Explain the drill, demonstrate the block desired, and designate one line as blockers and the other as opponents. After several practice blocks, have the blockers become the opponents and the opponents become the blockers. During the course of the drill, emphasize the three phases of blocking: the approach, contact, and follow-through.

c.   Forward Passing Drill. Form the class in groups of ten men each. The groups form two lines with the men about ten feet apart and the two lines ten to fifteen yards apart. Using at least one ball to a group, practice grip, balance, throwing with a spiral, and follow-through. The ball is thrown by each man, in turn, to the next man in the opposite line who catches it and throws.

d.   Passing and Receiving Drill. Each of the groups is formed as for the drill outlined in c. above. One man, the center, is stationed between the two files with the ball. One file is designated as passers and the other as receivers. The center snaps the ball to the first passer. He passes to the first receiver who runs down the field at the snap of the ball. The receiver catches the pass and returns the ball to the center. Upon his return, the receiver joins the "passer" file and the passer joins the "receiver" file. This rotation continues until all men have an opportunity to throw and receive forward passes.

e.   Other Drills. If time permits, other fundamental drills may be included, such as snapping the ball from center, kicking, lateral passing, and other individual skills of a specialty nature.

OFFENSIVE FORMATIONS AND PLAY

a.   A nine-man team is recommended. Three offensive formations are suggested for this size team. Of the three formations suggested, the double wing-back is the best.

b.   To complete the instruction in offensive play, it will be necessary to insure that some member of the team can perform the individual specialties. These special skills are passing the ball from center, punting, free kicking for kick-offs, backfield pivots, handoffs, etc.

c.   Men like to develop their own plays and should be encouraged to do so. Time must be made available for them to practice such plays before using them in a game.

DEFENSIVE PLAY

The class should be shown several defensive formations. Four different ones are applicable for the nine-man team. The selection of a defense depends upon the opponent's offense. The 4-2-2-1 and the 5-1-2-1 are better pass defense formations than the 4-3-2 and the 5-2-2. The latter formations are weak "down the middle". However, the 4-3-2 and 5-2-2 are stronger against a running attack. If fewer men are employed on a team, the defense could be altered by eliminating either linemen or backs, as required.

ORGANIZATION AND ADMINISTRATION

a. The instructor may divide the class into teams from the roster or by selecting team captains who, in turn, choose the remaining members of their teams.

b. The officials may be assistant instructors or selected individuals from the class. It is suggested that there should be at least one official for each game that is played. Close supervision of play and strict enforcement of rules are necessary to prevent injuries from excessive roughness.

c. To insure the success of touch football in a physical training period, the teams should be organized into a class league to stimulate interest and competition, and to select the championship team.

d. There should be one ball for each fifteen men.

e. The area for practice and play should be grassed and level. The field should conform as nearly as possible to the size specified in paragraph 9a(1).

RULES

It is important that the participants know the rules that govern touch football. It increases the players' enjoyment in the activity, lessens the chance of injury, and results in an organized contest. Official National Collegiate Athletic Association football rules shall govern all play except those special rules pertinent to touch football, as stated in the following subparagraphs.

a. Rule I - Field and Equipment.
    1. Section 1 - Field. The game shall be played on a regulation football field with goal posts. When space is limited, the dimensions of the field may be reduced to 300 feet long by 120 feet wide.
    2. Section 2 - Uniforms. Distinctive jerseys, shorts, sweat suits, or trousers, and basketball shoes or regulation footwear may be worn. Pads, helmets, and cleated shoes are not authorized.

b. Rule II - Length of Game.
    1. Section 1 - Periods. The game shall be played in four periods each ten minutes in length, with a one-minute interval between the first and second and the third and fourth periods; and with a ten-minute interval between the second and third periods.
    2. Section 2 - Contest. By mutual agreement of opposing coaches or captains, before the start of contest, the length of the periods may be shortened or lengthened.
    3. Section 3 - Time Out. Time out shall be taken -
        a. After a touchdown, field goal, safety, or touch back.
        b. During a try for a point.
        c. After an incomplete forward pass.
        d. When the ball goes out of bounds.
        e. During the enforcement or declination of penalties.

c. Rule III - Players and Substitutes.
    1. Section 1 - Players (nine-man game). Each team shall consist of nine players. The offensive team shall have a minimum of five players on the scrimmage line when the ball is snapped. Note: The following diagram designates the position of the players -

END GUARD CENTER GUARD END

QUARTERBACK

HALFBACK HALFBACK

FULLBACK

2. Section 2 - Players (six-man game). Each team shall consist of six players. The offensive team shall have a minimum of three players on the scrimmage line when the ball is snapped.
Note: The following diagram designates the position of the players -

END   CENTER   END

HALFBACK HALFBACK

FULLBACK

3. Section 3 - Substitutions. Unrestricted substitutions may be made when
 a. The ball is dead.
 b. The clock is running, provided substitutions are completed and the ball is snapped within 25 seconds after the ball is ready for play.

d. Rule IV - Playing Regulations.
1. Section 1 - Starting the game and putting ball in play after any score shall be as prescribed by the NCAA Football Rule Book, with exception of Rule 4, Sections 2 and 3.
2. Section 2 - Kick-off. The receiving team, in a nine-man game, shall have three players within five yards of its own restraining line until the ball is kicked.
3. Section 3 - Restriction. In a six-man game, the only restriction on the receiving team is that all players must remain back of their own restraining line until the ball is kicked.
4. Section 4 - Fumbled Ball. A ball that is fumbled and touches the ground during a run, kick, or lateral pass play, may not be advanced by either team. The ball may be touched and recovered by any player. It shall be dead and in possession of the player who first touches it after it strikes the ground.
Note: Players shall be warned against diving on fumbled balls and may be penalized for unnecessary roughness.
5. Section 5 - Fumbled ball or lateral pass. A fumbled ball or lateral pass, intercepted or recovered before it touches the ground, may be advanced by any player.
6. Section 6 - Downed ball by legal touch. The player in possession of the ball is downed and the ball is dead when such player is touched by an opponent with both hands simultaneously above the waist and below the head.
7. Section 7 - Forward passing. One forward pass may be made during each scrimmage play from behind the passer's scrimmage line.
8. Section 8 - Eligible receivers. All players of offensive and defensive teams are eligible to receive forward passes. Two or more receivers may successively touch a forward pass.

e. Rule V - Fouls and Penalties. Section 1 - Use of hands and arms. For both offense and defense, as prescribed in NCAA Football Rule Book.

VOLLEYBALL

INTRODUCTION

a. Volleyball is a popular sport. The game entails much physical activity, yet it is not strenuous. It is, therefore, a game for young and older men alike, for beginners and for skilled players. It may be played indoors or outdoors on any type of terrain. As an informal activity, volleyball can be played by any number of men; as an organized activity, it provides, as few other sports do, a game for twelve men to play in a limited area.

b. While volleyball requires no great skill to play, it does permit a high degree of proficiency. A man naturally gets more enjoyment when he knows the game and plays it well. For this reason, instruction in the basic skills should be provided.

ORGANIZATION

Usually a ten to fifteen-minute period of instruction, followed by scrimmage during the first three or four classes is enough to teach the basic skills, rules, and techniques of volleyball. More time can be given to teaching basic skills, if available, but the emphasis is on competitive play rather than on formal instruction. It is best to lecture and demonstrate to the entire class, then divide the class into smaller groups for practice. For drills and scrimmages, divide the class so that there will be from twelve to twenty-four men to each court. One court may be used for instruction by allowing twelve players at a time to execute the drill while the other class members observe, act as coaches, or retrieve balls. After the instruction phase of training has been completed, divide the class into six-man teams. Organize the teams on the basis of ability. All teams should be as nearly equal as possible.

PLACE IN THE PROGRAM

Volleyball may be used occasionally as a competitive activity during the sustaining stage. It is a year-round sport, but it should be included in the physical training program only when it is impractical to conduct a more strenuous activity. It is an excellent self-interest activity.

BASIC SKILLS

a. Passing.

1. Handling the low ball. A ball that is lower than the waist is one of the easiest to hit, but is also a frequent cause of the fouls of holding or carrying the ball. The best position for handling a low ball is to have the feet staggered, knees flexed, and arms flexed at the elbows and rotated so the thumbs are pointing outward, the palms up. When the fingers contact the ball, the entire body reacts in a lifting motion. The arms and hands swing upward in a scooping action. It is important that the fingers, not the palms, contact the ball, and that the ball is batted, not thrown.

2. Handling the high ball. The chest pass is the most effective method of playing the ball. To receive the ball, the feet are staggered, knees are flexed, and the body is tilted forward. The elbows are raised sideward to a point in line with the shoulders. The wrists are extended in line with the forearm and the arms, wrists, and hands are rotated inward. To pass the ball, the hands are chest high, thumbs pointing inward. The fingers are flexed, forming a cup, allowing them to contact the ball. On contact with the ball, the wrists are snapped while the fingers and elbows are pushed upward, sending the ball upward. A high ball is much easier to handle than a low one.

b. Serving.

1. The underhand serve. Take a position behind the back line facing the net, left foot forward, holding the ball in the palm of the left hand. The left knee is flexed, the right knee is straight. Swing the right arm back and at the same time move the left hand (holding the ball) across the body in line with the right hip. Then swing the right arm forward hitting the ball off of the left hand with the palm of the right hand, raising the hips and arching the back in the same motion. Be certain to swing the right arm in a straight line, or the ball will be difficult to control.

2. Placement of the serve. When the opposition is in formation, the server should try to place the ball in the right or left back area, and not near the net.

    c. Setting up. A setup is a ball hit into the air near the net by one player, so a teammate may hit or "spike" it sharply downward into the opponent's court. The chest pass is the best pass to use. The ball is sent approximately ten feet into the air toward the spiker so it will descend from four to twenty inches from the net.

    d. Spiking. The spike is a leap into the air and a sharp downward hitting of the ball into the opponent's court. A spiker must be able to spring easily from the floor, judge the movement of the ball, and strike it with a downward movement of his arm. To jump from the floor, step off with one foot and jump with the other. Stand with the right or left side to the net, facing the setup man. Much depends upon the setup man to place the ball in the proper position. The spiker jumps into the air and strikes the ball above its center so as to drive it downward. A snapping movement of the arm and wrist will drive the ball forward and downward with power and control. Aim for a weak spot in the opponent's defense.

    e. Blocking. The block is a technique of defense used to prevent a spiker from driving the ball across the net. It is an attempt by one or more defensive players at the net to block a hard hit shot by using the force of the ball to send it immediately back into the opponent's court. An effective block is for forwards on the defensive team to spring into the air at the time of the spike, placing both hands and arms in the expected path of the ball. An effective block tends to upset the offense and presents another element for the spiker to worry about. To be effective, the blocker must anticipate the path of the ball and time his block with the spike.

DRILLS TO DEVELOP BASIC SKILLS
    a. Passing.
        1. Divide the class into twenty-four-man groups. Have them form a circle and begin passing a ball around the circle trying to prevent it from touching the floor.
        2. Divide each group with twelve men on a side facing the net. Form four ranks per side, with the first ranks passing the ball back and forth over the net until a pass is incomplete. Then have the second rank move up. Place the groups in a regular playing formation concentrating only on passing, using both the chest pass and the low pass.
    b. Serving. Break the men into two groups - one line to act as servers, the other as retrievers. Change over frequently giving each man a chance. When the men can control the serve, have each server try to place the ball in the various areas of the court.
    c. Spiking. Have two files on one side of the court facing the net. One file is the spiking file, the other is the setup line. One man from each file moves up to the net at one time. The spiker tosses to the setup, the setup sets the ball up for spiker, and the spiker drives it over the net. Rotate the files.

OFFENSIVE PLAY
    a. Each member of a good offensive team should -
        1. Be able to serve.
        2. Know the capabilities and weaknesses of each of his teammates.
        3. Have an understanding of all offensive plays.
        4. Be able to analyze the opponent's weaknesses.
        5. Always know what area of the court he is responsible for.
        6. Be ready to "back up" a teammate receiving the ball.
    b. The big offensive power is the spiker. It is also necessary, however, to build a well-balanced team that can serve, pass, and "set up".

DEFENSIVE PLAY

The reception and handling of serves and spikes is the primary duty of the team on defense.

  a. Receiving the Serve. The forwards move to the rear of their area. The left and right backs cover the rear, the center back plays slightly forward of the other two backs.

  b. Blocking. The block is made by the center forward and either the right or left forward. The forward not executing the block must cover the position left vacant.

ABRIDGED RULES

  a. The volleyball court is 30 feet wide by 60 feet long.

  b. The top of the net is 8 feet high.

  c. A volleyball team consists of six players.

  d. A match consists of the best two out of three games.

  e. The first team scoring 15 points wins the game, provided that they have two points more than their opponents.

  f. A deuce game is a game in which both teams score 14 points. The game is continued until one team obtains a 2-point advantage over the other.

  g. Only the serving team can score. If the serving team commits a fault, it loses the serve to the opposing team.

  h. The team receiving the ball for service rotates one position in a clockwise direction.

  i. The ball is put into play by serving from behind the back line.

  j. A served ball touching the net results in the loss of the serve. At any other time during play, a ball touching the net is still in play.

  k. The ball is out of play when it touches the ground or goes outside one of the boundary lines..

  l. All line balls are good.

  m. The players must hit or bat the ball; they may not throw, lift, or scoop it.

  n. A player may not touch the ball with any part of the body below the knees.

  o. A player may not play (touch) the ball twice in succession. In receiving a hard-driven spike, a defensive player may make several contacts with the ball even if they are not simultaneous. All such contacts, however, must constitute one continuous play, and all must be above the knees.

  p. The ball may be touched no more than three times on one side of the net before being returned across the net to the opposing team.

  q. A player must not touch or reach across the net.

  r. A player may not cross the line under the net; he may touch it, however.

  s. For complete official volleyball rules, see the United States Volleyball Association: <u>Volleyball Official Guide.</u>

———

CPSIA information can be obtained
at www.ICGtesting.com
Printed in the USA
BVHW011409120220
572173BV00007B/272